Once Upon A Boring Day
Written by
Kailyn Boyd

ISBN: 8-218-36192-1
ISBN-13: 979-8-218-36192-1

Table of Contents

Intro

This is a book filled with people's stories; the ordinary people around us who have worked hard to achieve where they are today or are in the process. But first, my story. Growing up, I was obsessed with reading. My mother tells me she knew she had a reader on her hands when I was just a little girl and she would wake up to the sound of books falling out of my bed after I had fallen asleep with them. I dove into these books in order to surround myself with the beauty of other people's thoughts. The sto-

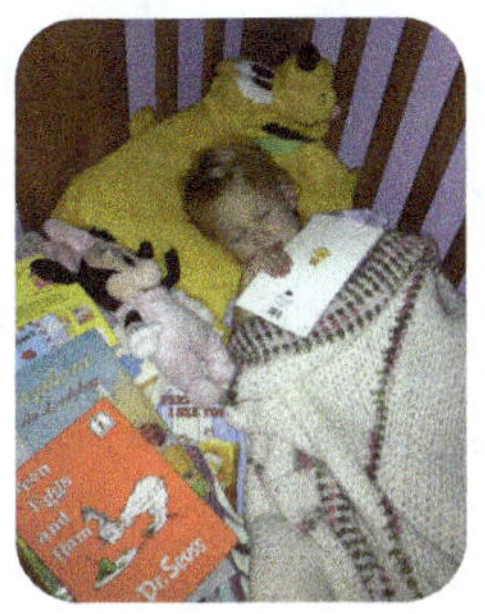

ries that made them the thing that I dreamed of becoming: an author.

My days growing up were spent watching Disney movies, making up dances to Taylor Swift songs with my sister, and reading Harry Potter with my dad. I was constantly surrounded with amazing people, people I looked up to all my life and will continue to for as long as I live.

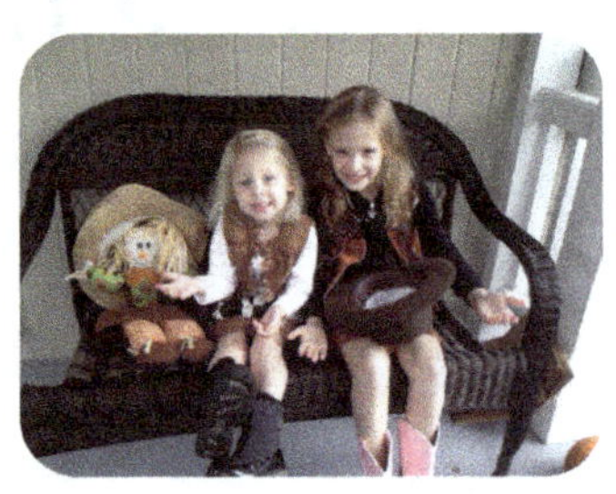

Getting older, things changed and it was clear to me. People around me got these prized possessions called phones. Hanging out with friends didn't consist of making iMovies or having dance parties anymore but instead we were making TikToks or staging pictures for Instagram. People now cared and even changed who they were in

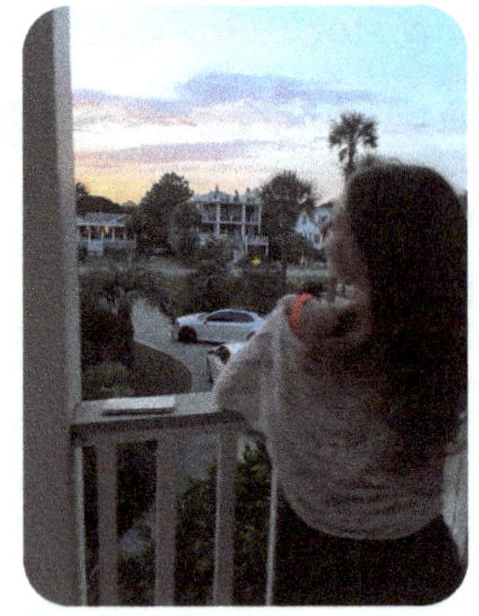

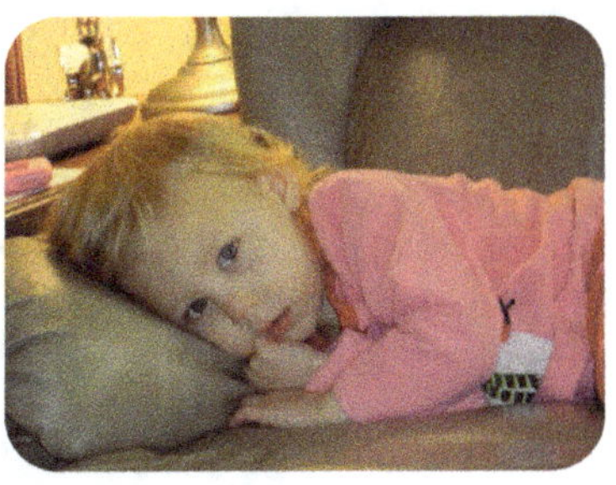

order to please people on their phones. I was their age and I saw the fun in social media but I have always been told I was mature for my age and even then I saw how different everything was.

My mom couldn't come up to me anymore and take a picture without me worrying how my hair looked or who she was sending that picture to. But why was I thinking this way when she was probably sending it to my grandma who didn't care if I had greasy hair while making a cake for my sister's birthday? When at the same time, everyone around was worrying the same thing even though they looked at a picture of someone else and didn't even notice they didn't wash their hair the day before?

I began to think about it. I talked to my dad who had grown up dreaming of becoming a Disney animator and had taken that dream to become an author on his own. We discovered something that would someday result in me creating the book you are reading right now. Those phones stop people from being bored. And though your parents tell you that you shouldn't be bored and to make plans, being bored is what leads to the creativity that gets you furthest in life. Walt Disney was probably laying on his bed one summer day bored when he saw his dog and thought it would be funny if his dog was best friends with that mouse he had been chasing the other day. Maybe George Lucas stared at the clock too long in class one day and instead of the hour hand he saw a glowing sword creeping up to when he could go home where he would expand that thought into a

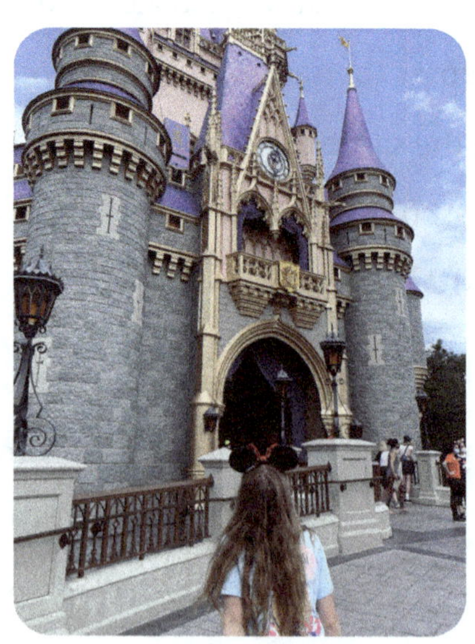

universe far far away. But kids these days don't have that. Bored at home? Facetime your friend. Bored in class? Play a game on your computer.

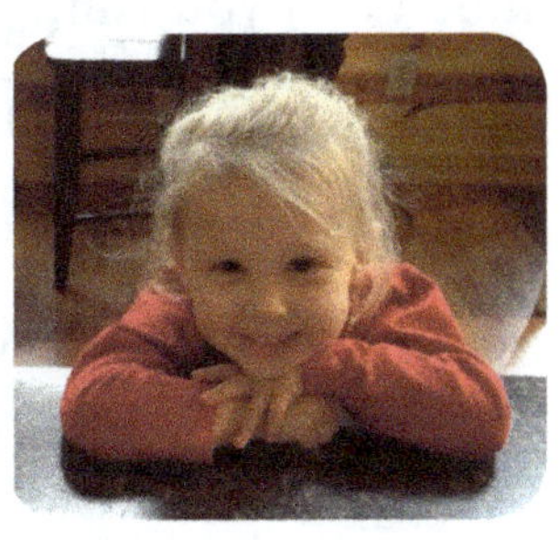

I have seen the extreme results of social media today and I am astonished by them but what if at the same time that social media is stunting our future winner of the Academy Award for Best Original Screenplay, all because these people aren't bored enough? It sounds crazy but in a way it makes complete sense.

So I took what I saw, combined it with my favorite thing in the world and created the book you are reading right now. I interviewed people from students to teachers to directors of companies to retired artists and asked them questions. About how they got to where they are today, where they hope to be, what role social media played in that, and what role creativity played in that.

I hope that in reading this book and in hearing other people's stories, that you will understand my crazy idea. Maybe this book will inspire you so much that you will become the next William Shakespeare! Or maybe you will read it and simply decide to put your phone down next time you have a free chance and instead pick up a guitar or a tennis racket.

Wherever this takes you, I hope you learn a little bit more than you did before you cracked the spine of this beautiful paperback.

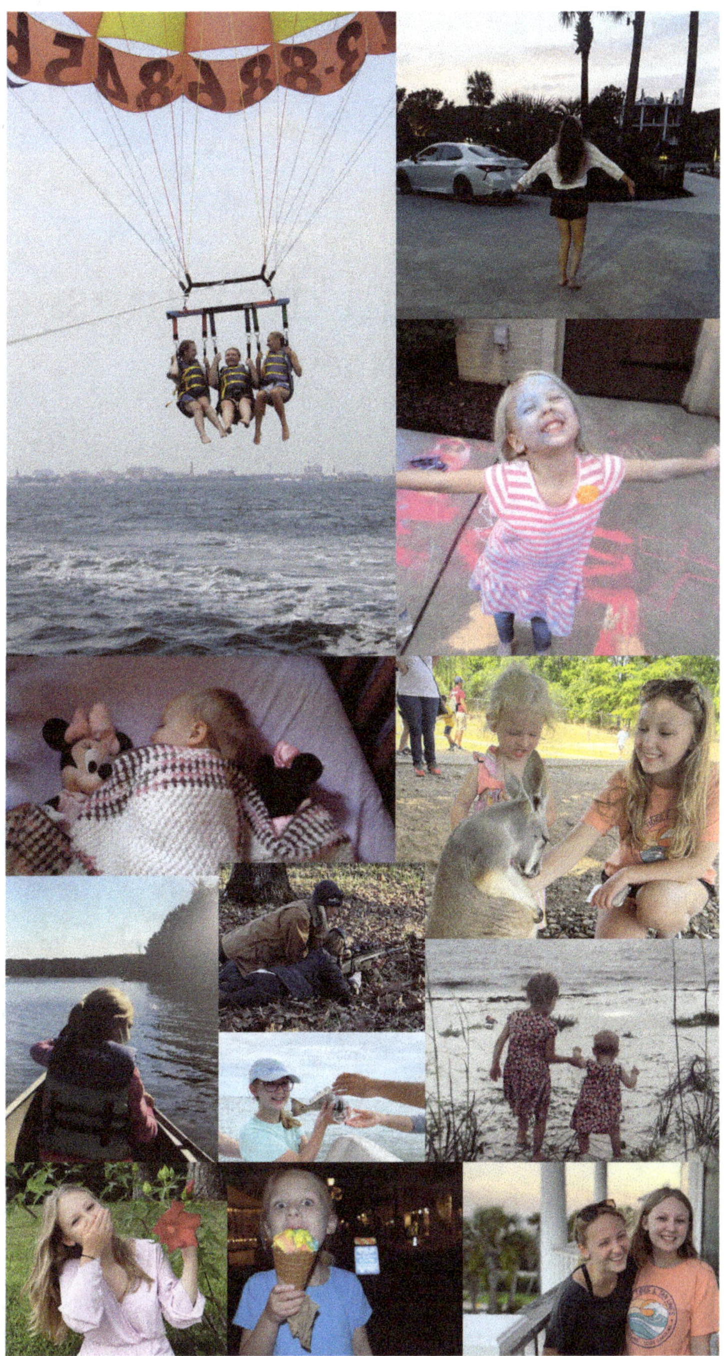

"10,000 bad drawings"
-Matthew B.

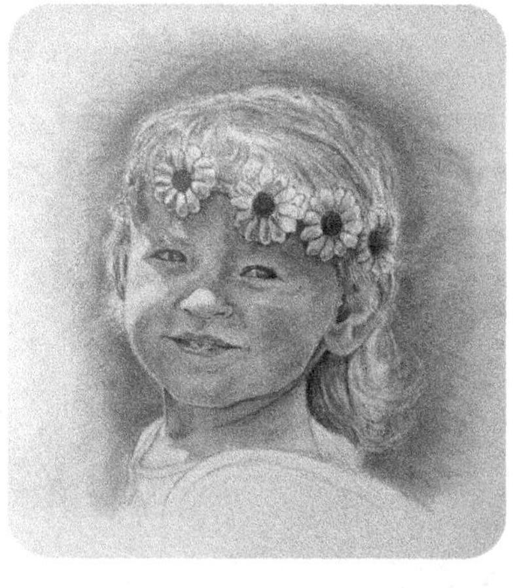

Matthew is a small business owner of two very successful companies, Evoke Design and MB Books. Evoke Design is a graphic design company he developed over 20 years ago. He spends his days working with clients to create out of the box solutions to whatever they ask of him. MB Books is Matthew's place to self publish his

6 childrens books, as he comes up with funny stories and illustrating them in creative ways.

Both jobs are extremely creative ways to spend your time, whether that's creating logos, websites, brochures, and ads or drawing a little sketch that leads into an idea to expand. Simple sketches are ways that Matthew spends his free time. Sometimes those lead into new ads, books or characters.

"I HOLD A PEN AND JUST START DRAWING LINES WITH NO IDEA WHAT I'M SKETCHING. SOMETIMES THIS LEADS TO A GREAT AD DESIGN, SOMETIMES IT LEADS TO A MESS OF LINES. I TRY TO TURN BOREDOM INTO SOMETHING POSITIVE."

For Matthew, there were two main things that pushed him to be creative. He grew up with dyslexia, making reading and spelling more challenging for him. During these hard times, he turned to art and creativity because of his love for drawing. The second thing was his time working at Disney for a college internship program. He worked as a janitor in Animal Kingdom. "This four and a half month pick-

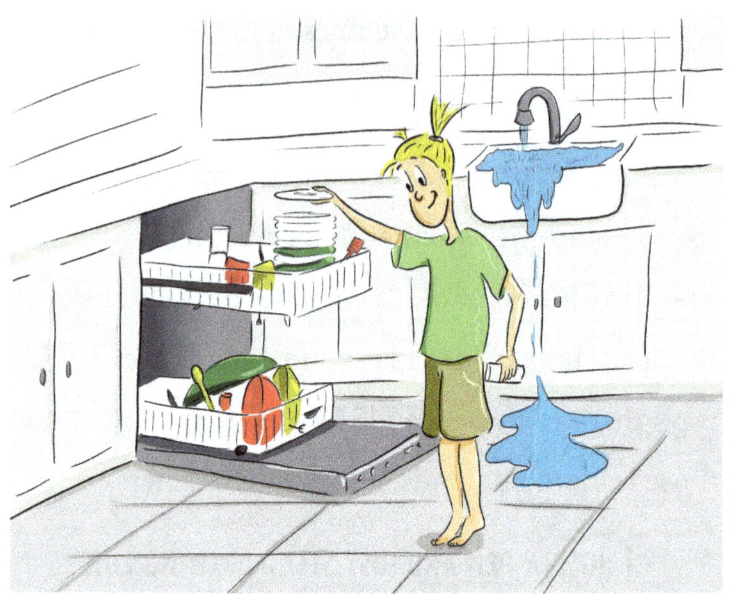

ing up trash really pushed me to work in a creative job." He explained how much he loved his job there but it wasn't very creative and he missed having that.

But when it comes time for Matthew to now begin to create something in his now very creative businesses, his first step is to not do it, but to clear his head and go for a walk, a drive, or the gym to work out. In getting his mind on something else, he finds the solution to whatever he was working on. And once he gets the idea, he takes a pen and sketches out his idea.

"THE SKETCHES ARE BAD DRAWINGS. I'M REALLY TRYING TO GET THAT IDEA FROM MY HEAD ONTO PAPER IN SOME WAY TO KEEP IT MOVING."

Next, he spends more time refining the idea to make it fully fit the proposed project given by his clients. "Sometimes the best ideas can come from a mistake. That's the great thing about being creative mistakes are sometimes what lead you down a totally new path that works out great."

"EVERYONE HAS AT LEAST 10,000 BAD DRAWINGS IN THEM SO JUST GET THEM OUT. KEEP DRAWING."

And clearly art is one of Matthew's favorite ways creativity is seen around him. Drawing either by hand or on the computer pushes him to improve and try new things. Art is in almost everything around you, whether it is a logo, animated movie, or the website on your phone.

Like many others, Matthew has a love-hate relationship with social media. As a pretty private

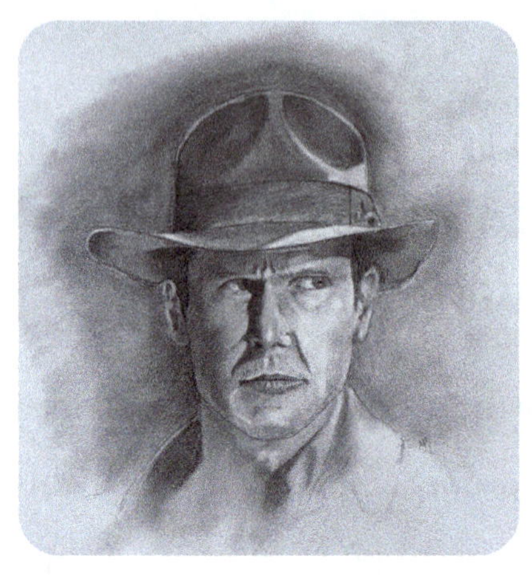

person he doesn't post often but he loves looking at other artists' creations. He also spends time on social media connecting with friends and family. If he does find himself on it too much, he tries to get up and do something else, telling himself not only to be a taker but also a creator. Matthew tries to only spend an hour or less on social media each day.

"I'VE TRIED TO TEACH MY KIDS TO NOT JUST BE TAKERS OF INFORMATION IN THIS WORLD BUT TO ALSO BE CREATORS. WRITE STORIES, MAKE UP YOUR OWN GAME OR GO OUTSIDE AND PLANT A TREE. IT'S GOOD TO LEARN AND HAVE INFORMATION BUT IT'S ALSO VERY IMPORTANT TO USE THAT INFORMATION AND CREATE SOMETHING WITH IT."

"Tapping into creativity"
-Olivia B.

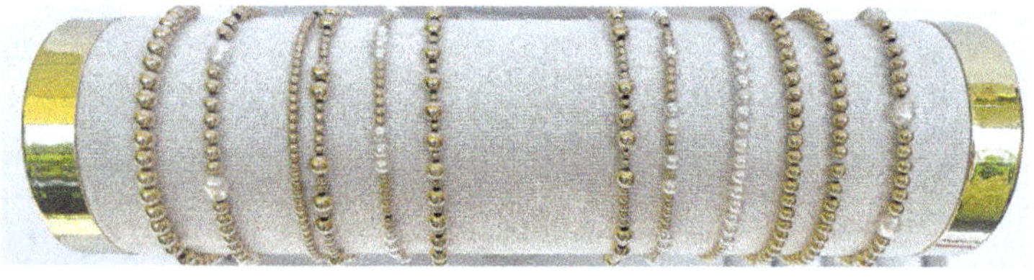

Olivia is a freshly graduated college student and now works at a national bank as an investment banking analyst. When I asked her how that job is creative, she explained how her job is very black and white with little room. Like many others though, she turned to her free time to find creative outlets.

And in this free time, she started out just on social media. Whether it was watching tv, tiktok, or planning time to spend with friends, she found that after a long day at work or school, social media was always a relaxing way to decompress. And one day she came across a video on tiktok of a girl making her own bracelets.

"THE GIRL WAS TALKING ABOUT HOW SHE ENJOYED PUTTING A SPIN ON THE DESIGNS OF POPULAR BRACELETS AND MAKING THEM HERSELF. THIS INSPIRED ME TO DO THE SAME AND I WAS COMPLIMENTED ON THE BRACELETS I MADE SO OFTEN, I DECIDED TO START SELLING THEM."

Since then, Olivia has been making bracelets and selling them in her free time. And because of this, she finds social media extremely helpful. It helped her to find the idea to do something that she now loves and probably never would've thought of on her own.

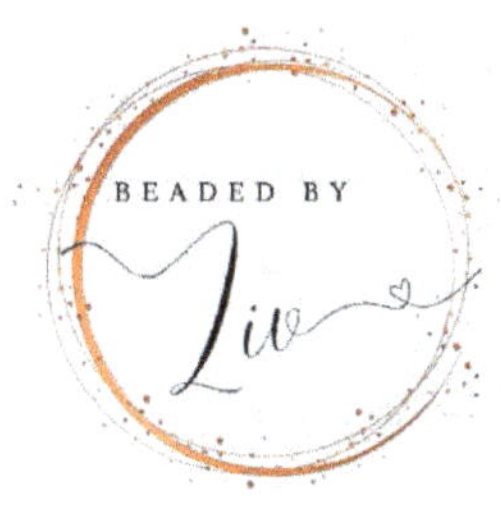

Even through all of this, she doesn't consider herself a very creative person. But whenever she gets stuck, taking a step back always helps her to clear her mind and get ready to jump back into the situation with a fresh mind. She says that keeping an open mind is necessary when it comes to creativity and that if taking inspiration from others and putting your own spin on it is what will get you started, then don't be afraid to do what will help you.

Olivia shared that this strong work ethic was taught to her by her parents. Getting good grades growing up was always a goal.

"BEING RECOGNIZED FOR GOOD EFFORTS AND STRONG WORK IS A BIG MOTIVATOR IN MY LIFE."

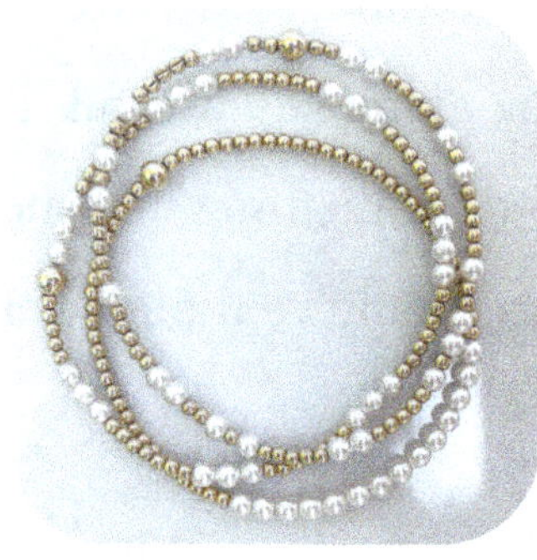

But even through all this positivity that Olivia sees in social media, she is very familiar with the negativity as well, saying that so many unhealthy comparisons are made the focus, which brings unrealistic expectations. She says that growing up she wished she didn't care so much about what people thought. Doing this can cause you to make decisions purely based on what others will like which can stunt your creativity.

But overall, Olivia is very thankful for social media. “I think social media can be a great resource and can be used to enhance one’s life in various ways. Platforms such as LinkedIn can be used to network in order to find a job or professional experience. Facebook and Instagram can be used to stay in touch with friends or family that you don’t see often. These platforms strengthen long distance relationships. Other platforms such as Pinterest or TikTok can be used as inspiration for recipes, crafts, workout routines, etc.”

“I think that social media has benefited my life overall. From connecting with people to getting inspiration for ways to be creative in daily life, I have seen a lot of things come out of social media for me. However, I also have experienced the comparison and struggles that can come from using social media in the wrong way.”

“I THINK THAT INSTEAD OF PROMOTING A DECREASED USE OF SOCIAL MEDIA, SOCIETY SHOULD BE PROMOTING HEALTHY WAYS TO USE IT.”

"What people post"

-Julia F.

Julia is a busy person. As a 10th grader in high school, she spends a lot of her time in sports, doing school work, working, or art. She says that when she is doing art, it gives her something to do with her hands, something for her to be proud of. And sports gets her mind completely off the internet and into the moment. But when she has a slow day, she loves to spend time with her friends and family, saying it really calms her down and helps her to decompress.

"I'VE CREATED LASTING MEMORIES THAT I THINK UPON AND COME TO APPRECIATE MUCH MORE THAN THE TIME I'VE SPENT SCROLLING ON MY PHONE."

Julia says that social media is an amazing tool but is often misused. "Everything man has created can be applied like this, but the internet was a groundbreaking invention that still has its pros and cons."

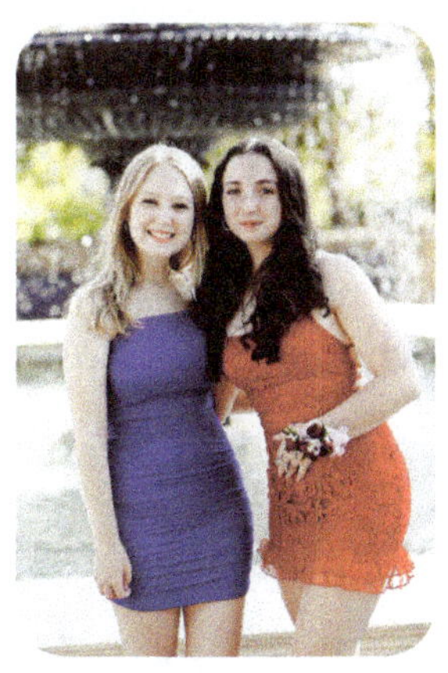

And with being in high school, she sees firsthand the differences of the people around her every day at school from what they post on social media. "I've seen how people change, and their appearance online becomes more important than who they are in real time. What people post does not fully represent who they are and they change themselves to fit certain standards we've put on ourselves."

Julia is a very athletic person, doing sports like flag football, volleyball, beach volleyball, track and field, and baseball. These are the things that she is proud of, the things that motivate her and keep her wanting to do more. And throughout her last years of high school, she will work toward more of those goals as well.

"I AM ALSO PROUD OF MY ARTISTIC SKILLS, LIKE THINGS I'VE PAINTED AND MADE WITH MY OWN HANDS."

While coming up with creative ideas, Julia regularly talks to the people close to her, to get ideas of how to start if she is stuck or how to improve in what she has done. "When I have no one to talk it over with, I'll talk out loud, hearing my own ideas will help me to create new ones."

As far as social media goes in Julia's life, she wishes she wasn't so dependent on it. But she wishes the same for everyone else as well.

"I SOMETIMES SHOULD GET OFF MY PHONE TO MEET THE REAL PEOPLE IN MY LIFE, NOT JUST THE VERSIONS I SEE OF THEM ON SOCIAL MEDIA."

"Mad at myself"

-Joy B.

Joy is a reading and math tutor who works from home. She sees young kids from kindergarten to fifth grade that are referred to her by their teachers, psychologists, or friends. She helps struggling readers or kids with ADHD or Dyslexia, that need that extra push of support from Joy.

"EVERY CHILD IS DIFFERENT. THEY HAVE DIFFERENT STRENGTHS AND WEAKNESSES THEY BRING TO THE TABLE."

Just like a normal teacher, Joy has to get to know each of these children. But differently than a normal teacher, she has to pick out each of their strengths and weaknesses in order to find the way they can learn each necessary piece of information. Creativity comes in at this point to find fun and engaging ways for these kids to overcome those weaknesses.

Growing up, her father rarely watched tv. She told me how he was always in the garage or house working on his next project. But her mother watched a lot of tv. Their TV only got 5 stations so there wasn't much to watch until MTV. With no other electronics, it turned into music videos 24/7. "I think that may have been the beginning of a time when you could always be entertained if you wanted to." She says now she wishes she would have controlled the amount of TV she was watching back then.

"IT IS A SLIPPERY SLOPE, BECAUSE YOU GET SO USED TO THE NOISE THAT YOU FEEL UNCOMFORTABLE WHEN THERE IS NO NOISE."

But now there is a lot more added to that equation. A lot of it being social media. Joy finds herself having to put away her phone when it comes to creating something. She has to get in the right mindset which means removing all distractions and making sure you are well-rested and not hungry. When your phone or devices are in view, it can be easy to get sucked in when you mean to be on it only for a second.

"I LOVE ARCHITECTURE. I AM SO INTERESTED IN DIFFERENT STYLES AND FUNCTIONS OF DESIGN IN LARGE SPACES."

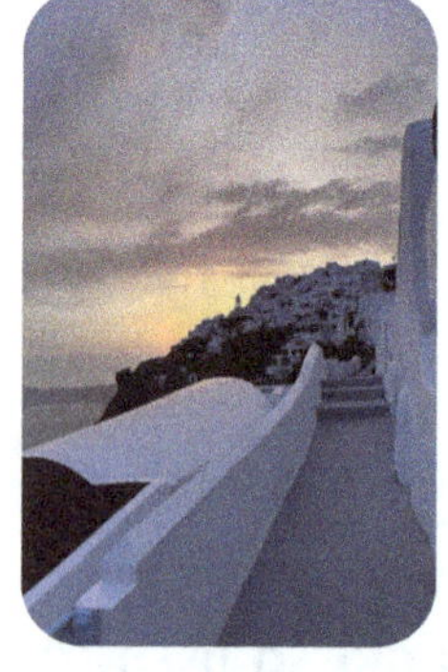

Because of this love for architecture she finds herself traveling around the world and seeing versions of architecture in so many different environments.

Joy shared that many times she gets mad at herself for spending too much time on social media but loves using it to connect with friends far away or to learn new things.

"I THINK IT IS GOOD FOR KIDS YOUR AGE TO THINK ABOUT SOCIAL MEDIA AND HOW IT AFFECTS YOU, YOUR MENTAL HEALTH, AND YOUR PRODUCTIVITY. WHEN YOU ARE AWARE, YOU CAN MAKE POSITIVE CHANGES."

"Magical Fairy Dust"

-Faith M.

Faith M. spends her days as a stay-at-home mom, author, and editor. Creativity is shown constantly through playing with her kids, reading her favorite books, writing books or articles, or reviewing people's work. She uses the creativity she has to help people expand and improve on their writing.

In all three aspects of her life, creativity is wildly shown. Faith explains, "There's a lot of creativity in being a stay-at-home mom. I play pretend, tell stories, and come up with fun activities for us to do. As a writer, I get to create characters, worlds, and narratives out of my imagination. As an editor, I get to think about how to make someone else's writing better, which is often a creative process."

When it comes to being bored, she reads or checks social media. But Faith has a personality like many others, who doesn't like being bored. She says she tries to find activities to do and does her best to avoid being bored. But she recognizes that sitting alone with your thoughts can lead to even more creative ideas.

"PEOPLE OFTEN TALK ABOUT CREATIVITY AS IF IT'S THIS MAGICAL FAIRY DUST THAT JUST SORT OF FALLS ON YOU AT RANDOM. BUT YOU HAVE TO WORK AT IT."

The extremely creative author, editor, and stay-at-home mom knows and shares how creativity is truly a journey that will expand the more you work at it. When you have a talent, it is up to you to show how, when, and if you will show it to the world. Faith advises everyone to set time aside each day for

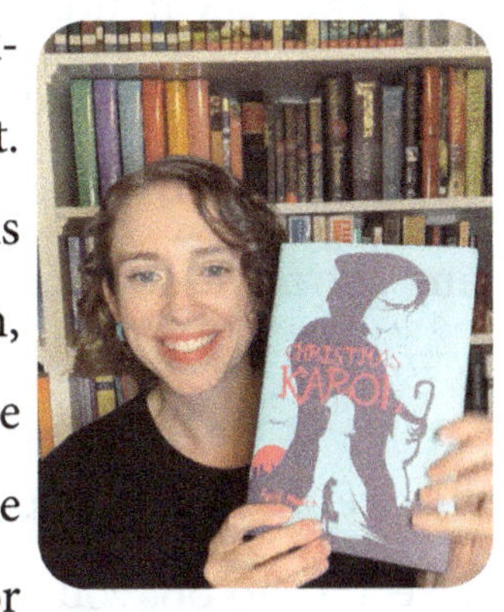

your creative talent, even if you aren't sure what to do with it.

"I COULD NOT LIVE WITHOUT STORIES. I LOVE THAT THERE IS ALWAYS ANOTHER BOOK TO READ. AND THAT PEOPLE KEEP COMING UP WITH AMAZING STORIES TO TELL."

Everyone has something that got them where they are today. And for Faith, her parents were big enforcers of meeting deadlines. Growing up with that, she now knows how to effectively plan out her work to stay on track. So when she has work to complete, she sets aside her phone, along with social media and any possible distractions and gets to work. When she is writing, she has a hard time getting started but after a while she figures out what she wants to do. She does wish she could've learned self-discipline earlier, but now she thrives knowing the importance of sitting down and making yourself get work done.

Doing this can also make you feel more productive and feel better about yourself. When you have a lot to do, you can feel stressed or anxious. It is so much healthier to get yourself into the habit of getting work done when you get it and setting aside distractions. If you get stuck, taking breaks and refreshing your mind is what lots of people, including Faith, do.

When it comes to social media, Faith explains that she often ends up on social media when she is procrastinating. Just like millions of others, she gets sucked in and ends up being on there longer than intended. But she says setting those separate times in her day for getting work done, really helps her control her intake on social media.

She says the healthiest way to use social media is to connect with people and to get your work out in the world. But about fifteen minutes is all she needs but says all different people need all different amounts of social media each day.

"Sticking close to my people"

-Katherine B.

Katherine is a 10th grader who has seen the extreme outcomes social media causes on her and the people around her. It is so easy to get yourself wrapped around social media and overthink everything you see. Katherine says one of the most destructive forms of social media is Snapchat.

"SNAPMAP CAN REALLY MAKE PEOPLE FEEL LEFT OUT AND CAN CAUSE A MAJOR EFFECT WITH MY MENTAL HEALTH BY SEEING PEOPLE HANGOUT TOGETHER AND STUFF. IT IS ALSO SUPER CREEPY BY BEING ABLE TO SEE WHERE EVERYONE'S LOCATION IS."

To Katherine, snapchat has affected her mental health in really scary ways. But she does her best to spend time away from it, as well as TikTok and Instagram. She does this by playing the ukulele or going on runs with her sister, her mom, or by herself. And in doing this, she finds a safe spot from social media. If something is bothering her, she talks to her mom or her friends.

She sees things like people posting pictures of others on their private stories just to talk bad about them. But Katherine understands how wrong that is, "It makes me feel terrible how low of a person you can be to do that."

"I AM MOST PROUD OF WORKING MORE ON MY MENTAL HEALTH AND JUST STICKING CLOSE TO MY PEOPLE THAT CARE THE MOST ABOUT ME."

"I've realized that you're not always going to succeed by getting all A's or by doing well in a sport but by just simply living everyday like it's your last and getting my mental health in check is something I am so beyond happy for that I've achieved so far this year."

And what got her to this point was music. She loves how it is such a beautiful way to express their creativity and tell others how they feel. Events in the world like Taylor Swift's Eras Tour, has taught Katherine how to embrace this music and how it can make her feel understood and cheer her up.

When doing projects, she starts off by getting inspiration from the people around her. She told me how she has learned that you have to show your creative side in order to inspire others in that same way. If your mom or your friends never did creative things, it would be harder to begin yourself.

And though Katherine has a good support system behind her, she wishes that throughout her life she could've kept more of her past friendships.

"EVEN THOUGH I KNOW GOD ALWAYS HAS A PLAN AND ERASES MANY PEOPLE IN OUR LIVES FOR A REASON, I STILL HATE HAVING TENSION WITH ANYONE SO I WISH I COULD JUST RELIEVE ANY TENSION I HAVE WITH ANYONE."

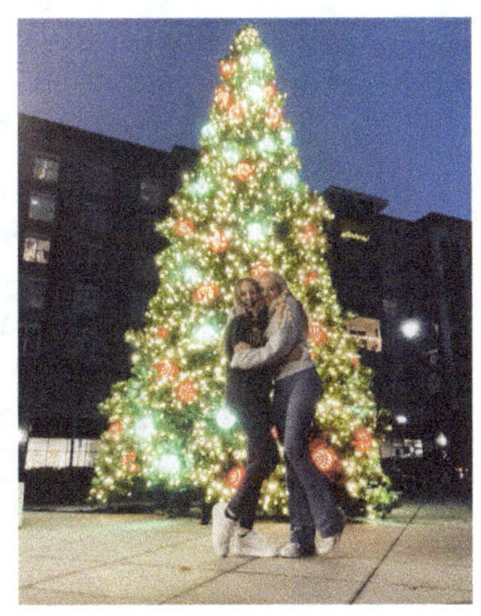

And the last thing she said that she has learned throughout her life, is to be kind to everyone, even your worst enemies.

"Adapt, smile and move on with the new normal"

-Virginia B.

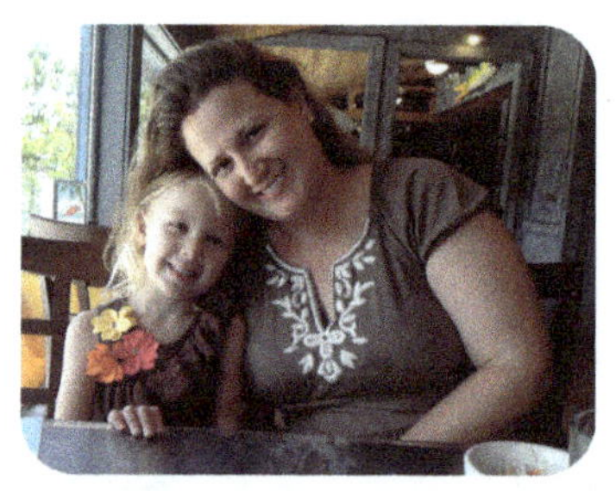

Virginia is another person who has multiple jobs, each that shows creativity in different ways. She explained to me her 3 main jobs in life: a mom, a dental hygienist, and a CPR instructor, all jobs critically important to the health of people around her. As a mom she spends her time "trying to keep her kids alive" and working to form them into good people and functioning adults.

And as a dental hygienist, creativity is shown constantly throughout her day, but in ways you might not expect. She sees all different types of people from different parts of the world with all different backgrounds, so each day she has to adapt to each patient. Her main job is to work with her patients in order for them to have a healthy mouth and body. But to do this, the person must be willing to listen to what she has to say, meaning she has to be what each person needs in that moment so they can listen to the imperative things she is telling them.

"HOW WILL I RELATE TO THIS PATIENT THAT PROBABLY DOESN'T WANT TO BE HERE WITH ME AT ALL? ARE THEY ANXIOUS? ARE THEY AFRAID OF THE DENTIST OFFICE?"

Once she discovers their overall vibe, she makes notes about each person. "I find what I call the emotional treasure for each patient, make notes, and be sure to ask for updates on their family. Some people like to talk about vacations, others their children, and some request no talking at all. Some people prefer different flavors or colors for their toothbrush and some people prefer their personal assistant to make decisions for them so they can continue their conference call during their dental appointment."

"Some people even bite my fingers because they are scared and forget where they are due to mental illness. I must treat each patient differently due to their circumstances of health, preferences, and attitude. I must creatively make decisions to make their session with me motivational for their home care and beneficial with my removal of bacterial debris present." Though on paper, her job is to clean their teeth, take x-rays, and tell you problems they need to get fixed, it is so much more. She explained to me how a dirty mouth and unhealthy teeth can cause heart problems or even death so even if a patient comes in screaming at her, she knows it is her responsibility to do her job because she cares for each person that walks through the door.

And in doing this job for many years, she realized the importance of saving lives. This realization led her into becoming a CPR instructor. And now her trick as a dental hygentist is brought into homes, offices, and places all over her town with so many more people. She shapes each CPR class around the people she is teaching. If she sees someone with a broken arm, she uses that as an exmaple in her class. If she has a group of young girls, she combines her usual first aid classes with babysitting skills to help them understand how to keep young kids safe they are responsible for. If it is a bunch of adults she knows have taken CPR classes before, she knows she just needs to give them a good refresher.

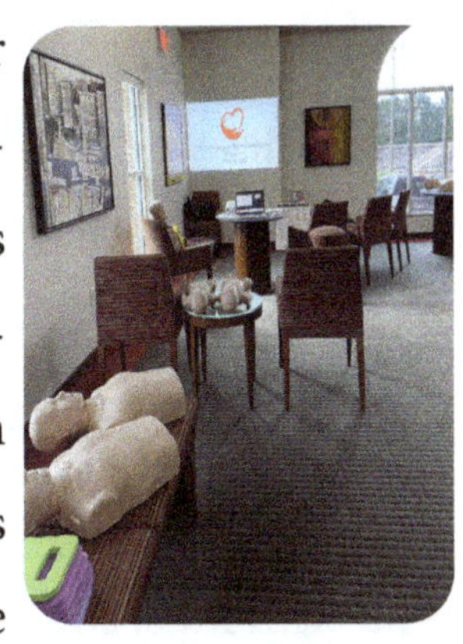

"I MUST ROLL WITH THE CLASS AND PICK UP ON ANY CLUES AND SENSITIVITY EACH STUDENT MAY HAVE. WE NEVER HAVE A CLASS THAT IS THE EXACT SAME. LEARNING LEVELS MAY BE A 3RD GRADER OR I MAY BE REFRESHING SKILLS OF A DOCTOR OF 20 YEARS."

She teaches them all compressions, how to use an AED, and even act out scenarios with young kids. She even takes into account the history of the people in the room. Depending on if they have lost loved ones, there could be more sensitivity or questions. When the class is first planned she learns things like how many there will be in the class and what ages they will be ranging from. During the class she answers their many questions and "what ifs…". And with kids, she will then make lunch with them, teaching them home etiquette, like what foods toddlers can eat, choking rescues, cooking safety, and cutting skills.

"USING CREATIVE SOLUTIONS, I'M ABLE TO KEEP THE ATTENTION OF MY STUDENT AUDIENCE SO THE PROPER LIFE SAVING TECHNIQUES CAN BE TAUGHT."

In doing all of this, she rarely has time to be bored. She explains how she doesn't like to be bored because it leads her into overthinking and worrying about whatever is going on. Even if she is sitting down to watch tv, she tries to spend that time doing something productive such as folding laundry, doing bills, or scrapbooking. "I think it's so important for each person to learn what to do when they are bored.

Some of the best creativity comes from trying something new."

To get herself productive, she makes lists and loves crossing off things she has accomplished. As a kid, she was taught the importance of good grades by her parents but they also taught her the importance of not only knowing the answers, but understanding each concept completely. They would sit down with her to help her tackle problems she didn't fully understand.

"I ALWAYS THOUGHT THAT I WAS NOT THE SMARTEST PERSON IN THE GROUP BUT I HAVE THE ENDURANCE TO PUSH THROUGH HOURS TO UNDERSTAND THE NEW MATERIAL. I ALWAYS FELT I WORKED THE HARDEST TO GET MY GOOD GRADES AS OTHERS IT CAME NATURALLY."

All that studying and working hard as a child worked out for her though. She became one of twenty-four to be accepted into the Denial Hygiene Program at college. She knew she needed top grades as people wait on that list for years.

"I'm not very creative in terms of artistic projects." She does enjoy looking at Pinterest and finding fun projects to do. One she found was writing down details about each patient she has seen instead of keeping it in her head like she used to which has made her life more structured and puts her more at ease. Before each day she reviews her list of patients, which prepares her for the next day.

As far as social media goes, Virginia calls it additive. Though she sees the good, she has a big concern for people of all ages spending too much time on it. "Too much of a good thing can be bad. Too much water and you could die. Not enough water and you could die." She explains jealousy produced by social media in one of the best ways I have heard. "People post all the good things about their life. You follow people and see all the success but not the 3am working on the project. You don't see every failure that was attempted before the big job hit. You don't see the years of hitting the books and long nights studying instead of partying to meet their goals. Everyone has different difficult challenges that go unnoticed by others. Sometimes social media can appear that you are alone in your challenges. Lastly, the unending battle of getting the highest number of "likes" from your followers creates an endless need to keep checking your posts over and over."

Virginia enjoys using social media to keep up with family and old friends. She also appreciates YouTube and how they have almost every solution to any problem like fixing something, learning guitar, doing physical therapy. As far as other social media, you can learn new recipes and see what's on sale, promote your business and research other businesses. But with everything, you must use self-discipline in order not to overuse it in an unhealthy manner.

"From concept to creation"

-Ron S.

Ron is part of a graphic design group as the director of digital services. "I manage day-to-day operations in Prepress, Large Format, I.T., and Marketing. I enjoy most aspects of my job but being able to work on marketing for the company allows me a creative outlet and is very fulfilling."

A big part of his job is just to solve problems. "Whether it is fixing bad design files, repairing a malfunctioning piece of equipment, or working and reworking schedules to ensure projects are completed on time. Being responsible for our company's marketing, both printed and online, requires creativity as well as business knowledge. For some projects I work with outside designers and others I do completely myself from concept to creation."

His dad was the one to show him the work ethic that works best for him. "If you want something, you have to work for it then you can achieve anything." Ron didn't truly learn this until college. His dad had a medical problem that made it impossible for them to pay for his college. That landed the entire college financial responsiblity on Ron. This made him work extremely hard to not only pass his classes but excel in what he could do.

Now Ron is constantly working with clients, having to think out-of-the-box in order for his ideas to succeed in his clients favor. That process is begun by taking notes and being able to fully understand his clients goals, concerns, and budgets. Then he is able to determine solutions that fit completely with the creativity his client needs.

When he is not working, Ron spends his time reading books, working on one of his antique cars, or playing a game on his phone.

"I THINK BEING BORED OCCASIONALLY IS NECESSARY TO HAVE A BALANCED LIFE."

"If you are never bored, you are probably on-the-go constantly and don't have the time to "re-charge your batteries". Being able to sit down and just relax, and yes, be bored, is just as important as having a hobby."

And one of Ron's favorite hobbies is collecting and working on antique vehicles. "I look at some of the designs that were created in the 1930's - 1970's and get inspired. I am currently working on a 'restomod', which is taking an original car and modifying it to make it unique and custom. I just spent a weekend fabricating a number of parts to make them functional but much more aesthetically pleasing. This gives me a since of pride and accomplishment to have something no one else has because I helped to create it."

When it comes to social media, Ron has a very healthy look on it; that it is a way to connect with people and to share interests and information as well as giving a chance for good advertising in a company. At the same time, he does have many concerns with it, saying how addiction to social media can lead to many mental health issues. When people get addicted to posting, they post every single thing, things some people don't even want to see. "Social media has been a breeding ground for cyberbullying and a quick easy way to spread propaganda and false information."

"SURROUND YOURSELF WITH POSITIVE, HONEST AND LOYAL PEOPLE. YOU SHOULD NEVER HAVE TO WONDER WHO TRULY HAS YOUR BACK."

Ron finds it easy to step away from social media as well, turning to spending time with friends and family or working on one of his hobbies. He finds that he would much rather engage with people in real life than online.

"...makes my generation feel more unified"

-Olohi A.

Olohi is a 10th grade student who is very passionate about dance. In her free time she is either choreographing dances to her favorite songs, reading, working out, or crocheting. She is in high school as well so she spends a lot of time around social media.

"I THINK SOCIAL MEDIA CAN BE BENEFICIAL AS LONG AS IT IS USED IN MODERATION AND WITH GOOD INTENTIONS."

Social media connects Olohi to people who don't live close. She says that many trends on social media come up in conversations through people that she maybe has never even talked to which makes this generation feel more unified. No other generations have really been as surrounded by social media as this one. It really connects these younger people who see the good while a lot of older people don't see these benefits.

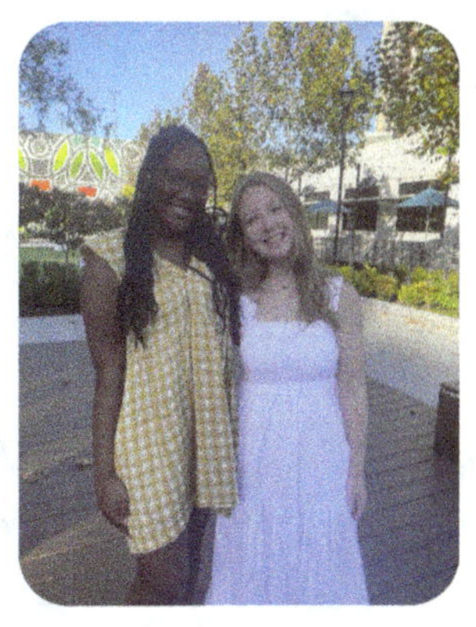

Olohi also finds creativity in the small things around her, like murals on the way to school.

"THEY ARE ALL SO DIFFERENT AND THEY SHOWCASE EACH ARTIST'S INDIVIDUALITY."

To begin projects of her own, Olohi starts by blurting her ideas out on paper. Doing this makes it easier for her to see what she is working with and what direction she wants to go with it. One thing that she wants to improve even more on is her dancing technique. She gets better by taking classes, learning from different choreographers, and strengthening in the gym.

"Try, try, try"
-Andrea T.

Andrea is a Chief Marketing Officer at a software company. She is a senior executive who leads and manages an organization's marketing strategies and activities. "They are responsible for driving brand awareness, customer acquisition, and revenue growth through effective marketing initiatives, market research, and collaboration with cross-functional teams. It's everything from brand, advertising, public relations, product marketing, creative, website marketing, lead generation, and social media."

Not only does this job require a creative mindset but also an analytical mindset. It is up to people like her to create the ads you see online, and each thing on that ad was creatively and logically planned out. The impact their design has on the viewer is a necessary thing to think about in order to find the best way to creatively tell people about their company and product. Doing this takes a lot of creativity and research.

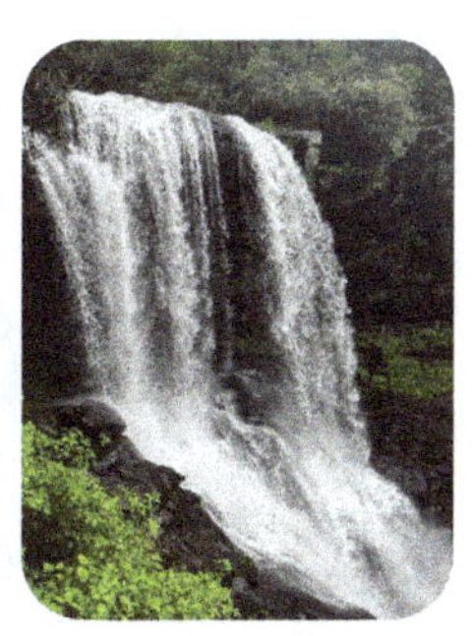

When Andrea gets bored, she spends her time going on a hike or going outside. If it is raining out, she will stay in and read a book, look at the news, or look at social media.

"BEING BORED IS A GOOD THING. IN TODAY'S WORLD WE ARE ALWAYS "ON" AND RUNNING."

She explains that being bored should be a time to rejuvenate and recharge your body and brain. The activities she does while bored help her to refocus and see things differently.

Her creative roots come from her parents, who encouraged her to think creatively and dream ideas. Her father is a musician and artist. Though Andrea didn't get those specific traits from her father, her parents' encouragement helped her to realize creativity can be used in ways other than artistically.

When beginning projects, she looks at other companies to get inspiration and lets her mind wander a bit. When I asked what advice to give people who are struggling with creativity, she said, "Don't be fearful to show something different or new. Be original. It's easier to be super creative and pull it back versus starting very narrow and trying to grow it. Try, try, try. Don't be afraid to try something. If it doesn't work, don't get discouraged, just try something else. Everyone who's creative tends to get stuck if something doesn't work. Remember it's all new learning and you can try something else. There are many virtual blank sheets ahead of you that can be written!"

And when she gets stuck, she sings or takes a shower. She says it is all about changing her mindset.

She sees this creativity in flowers blooming, house decorations, songs, movies, and pictures. All these things motivate her into that creative mindset needed to complete whatever she is working on.

When social media first came out, Andrea was on it a lot. She constantly got sucked into hours of looking at pictures or stories.

"WHILE IT HELPED INSPIRE ME, OTHER TIMES IT SUCKED ME DOWN A RABBIT HOLE WHICH MADE ME FEEL INADEQUATE. NOT PRETTY ENOUGH, NOT SKINNY ENOUGH, NOT PERFECT ENOUGH."

She uses the postive in social media to inspire herself. Or she researches what is going on in the world, but in doing this, she tries to remember that it is only one form of information and not the only information tool that can be used.

"I THINK OF IT AS LIKE A BALANCED MEAL, YOU NEED A LITTLE BIT OF EVERYTHING READING, MINDLESS ACTIVITIES, PHYSICAL ACTIVITIES, EDUCATIONAL ACTIVITIES – SO I TRY TO ENGAGE IN A LITTLE OF EACH... IT TAKES PLANNING AND DISCIPLINE."

"I lack creativity"
-Megan H.

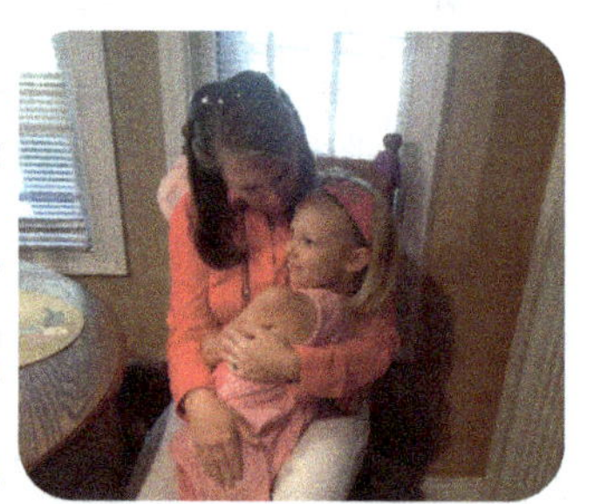

Megan claims to lack creativity but as a 4th grade teacher of 17 years, she has inspired countless children with different needs and unique abilities. She has seen it all, social media's rise in children and the good and the bad. With three very active children, she doesn't get bored often but knowing kids as well as she does, she knows the benefits of being bored.

"YES! I THINK BOREDOM IS A GREAT THING... IT FORCES CREATIVE THINGS TO HAPPEN."

Reading a book or taking a walk is how she spends her free time, but with driving her daughters to dance or cheering her son on during games, she doesn't get a lot of that. She explained to me how she had always been self-driven as a child, she pushed herself to get up and be active. She spends her days as a teacher forming lesson plans and using those to help guide herself to get through the curriculum her students need to learn. Her favorite ways creativity has been shown around her, she said, is displayed in how much she adores music and books in every genre.

"...AND HOW EVERYONE LOVES DIFFERENT GENRES FOR REASONS OF THEIR OWN."

Being a huge bookworm, I am the same way. Reading and music both bring their own senses of vulnerability. You are seeing into the minds of other people and each and every person likes different things for reasons we may never understand. These have two things in common, they both have different aspects that can align with any person. Different genres go with different people, personalities, and stories and Megan is not alone.

Social media has affected our world in every aspect. Megan uses the phrase that she got from a friend "Everything in Moderation" when looking at social media. As an elementary school teacher, no one knows better than her how to handle the approach of kids and social media. In her words, "I think children need to be mature enough to understand the damaging effects of it and MUST be monitored and have screen time..." she goes on to explain the importance of parents and educators teaching children to use it correctly and safely. Megan sets screen time limits for herself as well as her children to keep a healthy amount of social media.

I agree with Megan completely when she explained to me how time on social media differs for each person, that scrolling through social media shouldn't take precedence over important tasks with the expectation of people who use social media as their job. With being a teacher in the world of social media she has seen the good and bad with it all. Saying it definitely caused bullying with her students and that even though these problems happen mostly outside of the classroom, the students (especially so young) bring these issues to school. But through all that,

"IT ALLOWS ME TO STAY CONNECTED TO STUDENTS WHEN THEY ARE OLDER AND TO FOLLOW THEIR LIFE SUCCESSES."

Social media also gives her the opportunity to share things going on inside the classroom with the community. And outside the classroom, she uses social media to connect with family members that live far away.

"TAKE A BREAK AND A BREATHER."

So even a teacher of 17 years, who has acted as an educational guide for so many, claims to "lack creativity". But in reality, she has so much underneath the surface. These tiny things she does everyday, are her form of creativity and helps so many more than she probably even knows.

"Best ideas come from the mind in the moment."

-Ashlyn G.

Ashlyn is a sophomore who spends her free time with her family or friends or doing hair and makeup. While being in high school, social media has a huge impact on her daily life. As a teenager, she uses social media to communicate and keep in touch with classmates or people she doesn't see on a daily basis. She sees the importance of maintaining a healthy relationship with social media.

"IT CAN CREATE A FALSE SENSE OF REALITY AND EVEN AFFECT HOW YOU VIEW THINGS OR OTHERS THAT MIGHT NOT EVEN BE ACCURATE TO REAL LIFE."

Ashlyn says after too much time on social media, she sees herself comparing herself to others. But also she uses social media in a healthy way, to connect and meet up with friends. She pointed out the fact shown throughout high schools around the world; people aren't as scared to say things as they are in person. Ashlyn admits to having fights with family and friends through text just because people are more confident to say things to you when they aren't saying it to your face.

"YOU LOSE TONE ON TEXT WHICH CAN REALLY AFFECT A CONVERSATION."

Not just high schoolers deal with this though. People around the world are on both ends of this problem almost every day. It can be good at the same time.

When I asked my favorite question, Ashlyn said movies and music are her favorite ways creativity is shown in the world around her. But when it comes to motivation, the key for her is an open mind and confidence in herself.

"EYEBALL IT A LITTLE BIT BECAUSE I'VE FOUND THE BEST IDEAS ALWAYS COME FROM THE MIND IN THE MOMENT."

Proud of her kindness and good morals, she values creativity in every aspect of her life. Ashlyn is excited to learn lessons and to gain the ability to better look at things from others perspectives. With big dreams of taking a lifelong love of movies and transforming that into working in the film industry when she grows up, creativity means a lot to her. "I hope people continue to expand on creativity and let it become more present in our world." People all over the world dream dreams extremely similar to Ashlyn. They hope to take their favorite thing and transform it into a lifestyle. People who love to sing, dream of becoming world famous singers. People who dream of passing education down, become teachers.

"I generally don't get bored."

-Pace H.

Pace H. is a President and Chief Operating Officer of a very successful company. His job is to manage the real estate division of the company by planning, and building real estate assets around the southern part of the United States. This requires creativity to plan new developments or convert old buildings to new ones or even just raw land.

"I GENERALLY DON'T GET BORED; BORED PEOPLE DON'T UNDERSTAND HOW TO MANAGE THEIR TIME EFFECTIVELY."

While Pace takes a different approach to boredom, this is a very real viewpoint. As someone who has worked his entire life to manage his time in an organized way, rather than being bored, he needs no time of boredom to start creating. "I have generally been a self-started and highly motivated. I would not consider myself to have been a great student, but I did work hard and made okay grades, but I have always enjoyed working and have done so since an early age. I believe in setting goals and prioritizing objectives to reach those goals."

And with his job, he holds "creative work sessions" for most of the developments. His team meets face-to-face to throw out ideas until they settle on the best one. After that it is all about execution and delivery. When he is alone, those ideas come with quiet reflection, away from distractions, people, tv, and devices.

"...THAT ALLOWS ME TO COLLECT MY THOUGHTS AND THEN BRING THE WHOLE TEAM INTO THE PROCESS."

If he is stuck, that is a sign he needs a break. Either step back and take a walk or just push through it. "Usually you just have to 'start'". Nature is one of his big inspirations, so if it comes to it, a couple minutes outside can get Pace back on track.

As far as social media, Pace views it as a tool. He recognizes how addictive it can be, so to avoid that he puts away his phone at the same time every night and tries to spend only an hour on it each day. Social media helps him in his job a lot, like advertising, marketing and connecting with people.

"IT PROVIDES A QUICK, EASY, INEXPENSIVE WAY TO REACH A LARGE AUDIENCE."

"I get off. Period."

-Andria L.

Andria is a very creative person. She works for a government agency as a loan officer. When I asked what creativity comes with that job she responded, "Nothing of note, so I find my own creative outlets!" If you have a job that you feel doesn't bring out that creativity as you need, finding other outlets to express that creativity is such a healthy thing to do.

She really discovered what to do with that creativity. Sometimes, it is through photography, journaling, publishing her own journaling book for others, or mediation and yoga. She thinks boredom is good as long as you are using that time to find positive things to do. For example, she reads, journals, doodles, or researches about building a brand. Each of these things help her gain knowledge or fill her time with things she loves.

"I WILL SAY THAT MY PARENTS WERE OF A GENERATION OF GREAT WORK ETHIC, WORKING HARD TO GET AHEAD. CREATIVITY WAS AN OUTLET BUT NOT A CAREER."

She explained how both her and her sister overcame this concept in their own journeys. Her sister has been an apparel designer for thirty years and Andria is an entrepreneur and a professional photographer of fourteen years and doing more and more to expand this.

To begin her creative processes, she finds time and space for peace and quiet, for nature and meditation. She also finds time for art whether that is books, movies, or visual art, she finds inspiration from all of it. And she recommends using this trick as well. Find peace and quiet, then start the project.

She does wish she learned earlier that she is both analytical and creative. She said that learning these things involved a lot of self-discovery. She knew that whatever she would be doing in her life would be analytical but creativity involved from a career perspective was not supported or encouraged. She found a way that both could work throughout her journey. When she does get stuck, she likes to look through her old work to remind herself how wonderful her God-given gifts are.

"MEDITATION IS AN AMAZING TOOL TO QUIET THE MIND. GO OUT IN NATURE... THE COLORS, SOUNDS AND SPACE TO THINK, OBSERVE AND 'JUST BE' ARE QUITE POWERFUL."

She says that when she was younger she didn't appreciate nature as much as she does now. Children are such a wonderful way to see the creativity around you. "Our most honest creative selves show when we are children – endless imagination and the ability to dream without limitation, and observing the unfolding of nature."

"It's (social media) a gift and a curse. We are gifted with this incredible tool that has given us the entire world at our fingertips (information, knowledge, beauty, connectivity, etc). However the "curses" of being consumed by comparison, desensitization, and being bombarded with other people's opinions/group-think are just a few of the things that keep me aware and grounded about how I use my time on any social media platform."

"THE MINUTE I OBSERVE THAT I'M GOING DOWN THE RABBIT HOLE, I GET OFF. PERIOD."

She does use social media in healthy ways, such as posting uplifting content. She limits her time and keeps herself aware of the amount of time she spends on it. She doesn't look into comments and makes sure she looks up to remind herself how people look when they are sucked into their phones.

Though she spends about 2 hours on her phone each day, she admits that she doesn't know exactly a good amount for everyone. About an hour in the morning and an hour at night is mostly all she needs in order for posting, networking, and reaching out to other brands.

She has something a lot of people wish to have, the ability to just stop. When people get sucked into their phones they find it hard to just get off. But Andria gave some great advice. Step outside, see someone you love, or do something you love doing, then you can forget about your phone and focus more on what is going on in front of you.

"THERE IS A LOT OF INFORMATION OUT THERE – BOTH GOOD AND BAD – AND SURELY PROBABLY MORE THAN WE WERE EVER MEANT TO CONSUME. BE CAREFUL, BE AWARE, AND CHOOSE RESPECTABLE SOURCES AND EVEN THEN, EXERCISE YOUR ABILITY TO DISCERN TRUTH FROM FALLACY."

“Boredom is something I cherish”
-Karen C.

Karen C. is a Kindergarten teacher and a support specialist. She spends her time at her job playing games with kids and working to do creative things each day to inspire them. She knows firsthand what children in the next generation will be like. This requires focus and a lot of thinking out-of-the-box.

These kids are being raised with phones, tvs, ipads, and many more devices constantly surrounding them. So when they go to school, Karen is the one who has to pull them out of that and get them to really be engaged in books and learning. She finds joy in the little things like seeing the kids artwork.

"SITTING IN QUIET AND REFLECTING CAN BE A GIFT. BOREDOM IS SOMETHING I CHERISH AT THIS STAGE IN MY LIFE."

Obviously, with boredom comes the want and temptation to be on your phone more. When Karen finds herself being dragged into this rabbit hole, she tries to go on a walk or call a friend. Social media helps her to connect with past students and see a glimpse of their lives outside of school.

However, Karen thinks social media needs to be limited because it is often used as a comparison tool that can make you feel like everyone else's lives are perfect even though they are not.

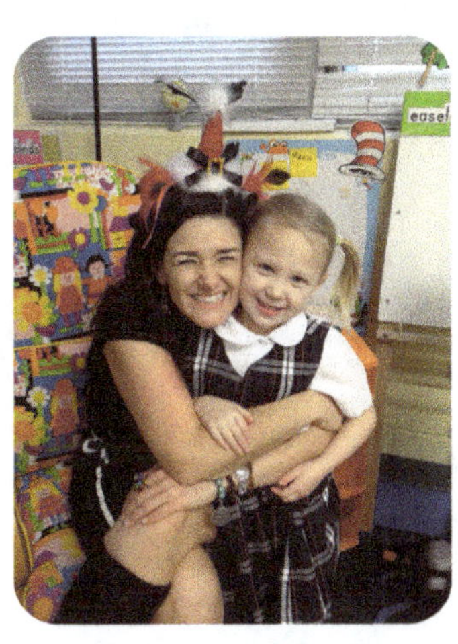

Karen has been a teacher for many years and has seen a lot during that time. The motivation and inspiration she possesses comes from her mentor and student teachers. She says they were the ones that really inspired her to bring smiles and energy into her job.

"I LEAVE THE DAILY STRUGGLES AND TRIALS AT THE DOOR AND WORK HARD ON SPREADING JOY."

"Make your mistakes quickly"

-Jim W.

Jim is an executive of a company that builds professional audio and video systems. This means it is his job to oversee projects when selling and installing audio and video systems for TV and media companies. So in his everyday life, he has to constantly use his creativity to look for technical solutions for companies to better their business.

When he is not working, he spends his time reading or learning something new. From working in his father's business growing up, he learned first-hand how important it is to be accountable for the work you do.

"MAKE YOUR MISTAKES QUICKLY SO YOU DON'T GET HUNG UP ON ONE IDEA. DON'T BE AFRAID TO TRY A NEW APPROACH."

When beginning a project, he takes some time to think about what the outcome needs to be and what the best approach would be to accomplish that. If he ever gets stuck, he pauses, sets a timer, and comes back after that time is up. Even in simple ways, technology is constantly part of his life.

"IN MY LIFETIME, PHONES WENT FROM BEING MOUNTED ON THE WALL TO BEING IN YOUR POCKET. HOW COOL IS THAT?"

Jim views social media as good in small amounts. Saying it can get overwhelming but that you can't let what is on it replace how you feel about yourself or others.

"Practice may not make perfect"

-Victoria L

Things like drawing, knitting, writing, playing violin, or playing video games are just some of the things Victoria turns to when she is bored. As a 10th grader who only spends about 15 minutes on social media a day, there is a lot we can learn from her.

She uses social media to find inspiration or to keep in touch with friends and family. She also sees how dangerous it can also be, saying, "it can also lead many to go down the dangerous rabbit hole of comparison, cyber bullying, exposure of mature topics toward younger audiences, and much more."

"SOCIAL MEDIA IS A DOUBLE EDGED SWORD THAT IS TO BE WIELDED CAREFULLY."

Victoria says that while sometimes it helps her to be inspired and get ready to be creative, other times it makes her feel tired and unmotivated to do anything but sit on her phone. For example, looking at other artists' work could make her feel inspired or it could start the cycle of comparison and could lead her into setting unrealistic standards quickly.

Victoria is proud of her commitment to God, and this has helped her to grow in her faith and also in other areas of her life. As far as the future, Victoria plans to go to college then move out of the country. In that time she wants to publish a few novels and do more with her creative passions.

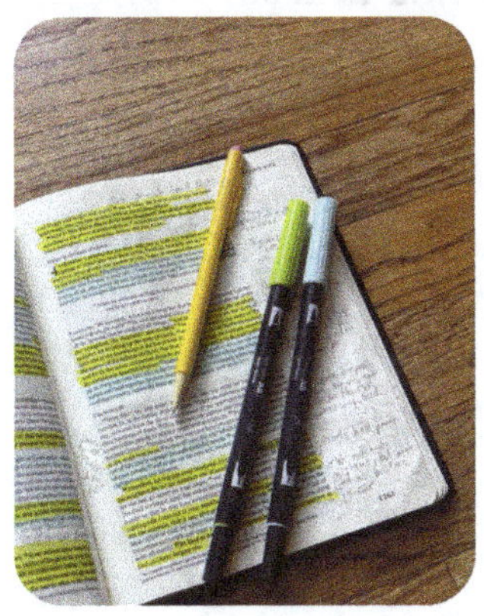

When beginning projects she prays for God to help her throughout the project or finds inspiration on Pinter-est. She loves to look around and see the beauty of the world around her. Creativity is constantly surrounding us and we just have to be present and take it in.

"EVERY LITTLE THING IS OF GOD'S PERFECT DESIGN, FROM SOMETHING AS SIMPLE AS A SUNSET OR CLOUD, TO THINGS AS COMPLEX AS A WHALE'S DESIGN AND HOW IT COMMUNICATES ACROSS SPANS OF OCEANS."

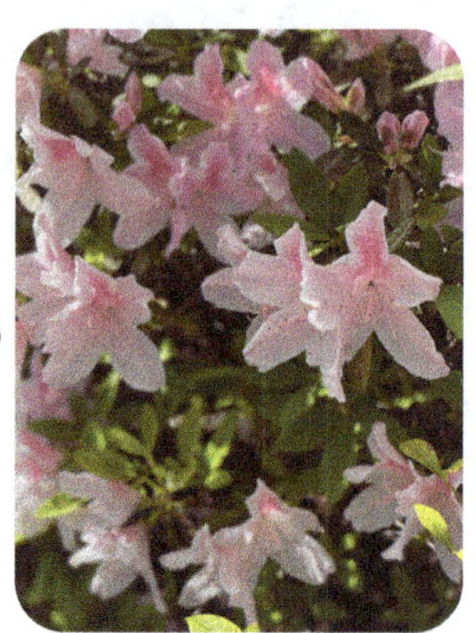

While not knowing exactly what she wants to do with her life, she knows she wants to spend time growing closer to God, by reading his word, praying, journaling, and even doing research to get closer to him in every way she can.

"PRACTICE MAY NOT MAKE PERFECT, BUT IT DOES MAKE PROGRESS."

"I miss the old days."

- Christina S.

Christina works at a place that preforms deep checks into companies. Her company helps other companies to prepare for these inspections. In doing this, her job shows creativity by requesting additions or changes to a company's performance so they can successfully improve their processes.

When it comes to doing these things, she starts by brainstorming with people on her team, then she will bring the idea to management which will hopefully help a company last longer.

Though she has been at this job for 6 years now, she still is learning things every day and advises people to never be afraid to ask questions. Especially when you are working, the more things you learn, the better at your job you will be.

When she is not working, she spends her time with her daughter, swimming, or taking a walk. These things help her to clear her mind and also give her a good intake of her family and nature throughout her day.

Christina told me that her parents were the ones to push her, support her, and encourage her to get on her own feet.

"GET UP, DRESS UP, ASK QUESTIONS, TRY TO ASSIST OTHERS IN THE ORGANIZATION WHO ARE ABOVE YOU. THEY WILL SEE YOUR INITIATIVE."

Christina grew up with this constant motivation to get out there so now that social media is big, she sees it as a double-edged sword. She talks about how easy it is to compare yourself to others on social

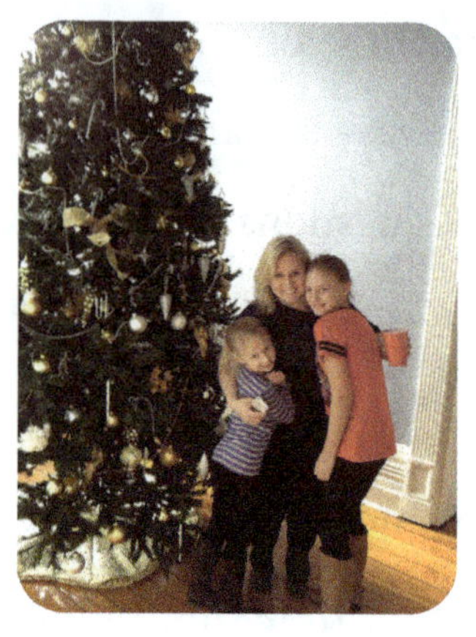

media but also sees what a wonderful creation it is because of all the wonderful things she learns through it.

If she is on it too much she tries to get off by going for a walk or cleaning, finding things better that she can do with her time. But social media can also help her find other things to do, such as finding new recipes or connecting with her long distance family.

"I WISH MY KID LIVED IN A WORLD WITHOUT SOCIAL MEDIA. I MISS THE OLD DAYS."

"More drama than you would think"
-Harper H.

Another dancer is Harper H. As a 9th grader, she spends her free time dancing, being with friends and family, making bracelets, or doing different hairstyles. But her favorite is dance. She is part of a competitive dance team so a lot of her time is devoted to dance. She also is a dance teacher for young kids, making up dances for beginning dancers.

"YOU TRULY HAVE TO THINK HARD ABOUT BEING CREATIVE TO COME UP WITH SOMETHING NEW THAT WILL LOOK GOOD IN A DANCE BUT IT CAN NOT BE A REPEAT FROM THE PAST YEARS."

As a smart kid who is a part of her high school's student council and was the recipient of the leadership award, she is smart about her intake of social media as well. She sees how overused it is and also how it is constantly used as a negative thing but feels it has so much potential for use in such positive ways.

She sees around her how much drama is created through social media. And she has seen firsthand how it affects her friends when it goes too far. She helps those people to talk to their parents and stop talking to whoever is treating them badly.

"MANY PEOPLE WILL SAY/DO THINGS THROUGH A SCREEN THAT THEY WOULD NEVER SAY/DO IN REAL LIFE. DOING SOMETHING THROUGH SOCIAL MEDIA CREATES A LOT MORE DRAMA THAN YOU WOULD THINK."

But Harper is a very responsible person who limits her intake of social media to focus on her friends and family and her passions. For example, when she starts projects, she starts like many others by drawing or writing down her thoughts to organize them and get started in the right direction.

Like many teenagers, Harper struggles with procrastinating. To fix that she says she can start doing a little bit of her projects at a time to limit the overwhelming amount she might have to do.

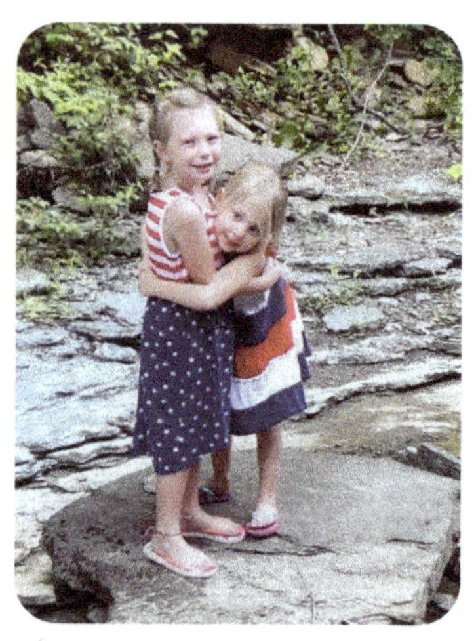

"It is proven that more calories are burned by reading and thinking"

-Angela T.

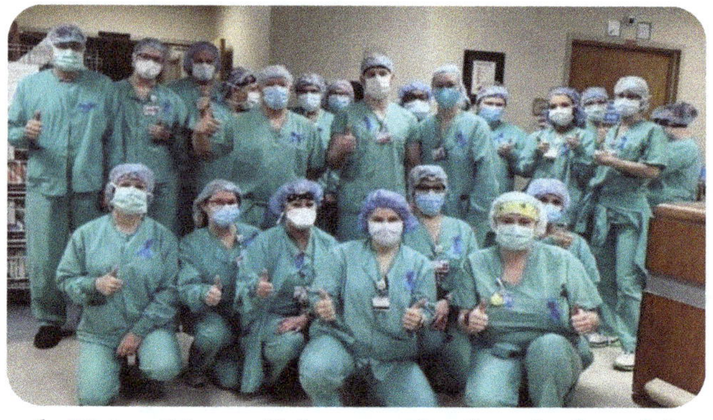

Angela T. is a Nurse Educator for Surgical and Sterile Processing Departments with a Bachelor in Science in Nursing and 18 years of experience as a Registered Nurse (RN). She describes her job as an RN as being responsible for patients having multiple surgeries done by different surgeons. For this, it is up to her and her team to meet the needs of the surgeons. This includes giving the right amount of medication, sterilizing equipment, and getting ready for the surgeon

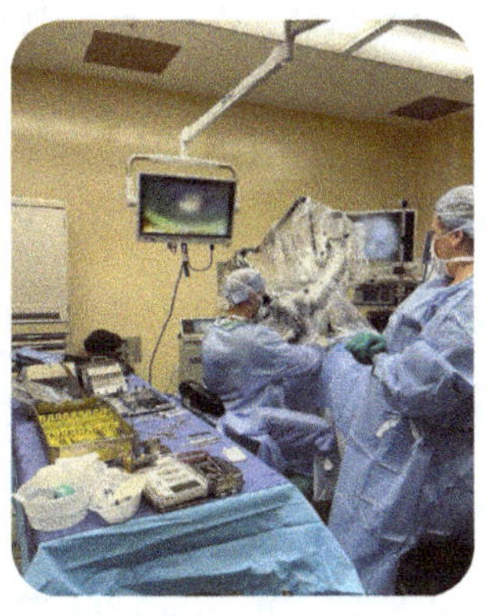

to come and to undergo a big surgery. It is nurses like Angela that stand by the patient's side, when they are in their most vulnerable state, in pain, confused, scared, and sometimes even angry. The nurse takes the patient back to the recovering room and get them back to full health in any way they can.

"I FEEL THE GREATEST JOB IMPORTANCE IS MY PATIENT ADVOCACY. IN OTHER WORDS, BEING THE EYES AND EARS FOR EACH PERSON AS THEY TRUST ME WITH THEIR LIFE AND WELLBEING."

This job is not an easy one, requiring full focus, efficiency, and preparation for anything to happen. It is Angela's job to oversee her team's action to provide optimal care and limited risks everyone involved. But for someone as creative as Angela, she felt her time spent in the OR everyday was smothering her creativity. "The atmosphere is stressful and the pace, fast. We are advised to be silent. We start each day by changing into blue scrub clothes and covering our shoes with blue booties, our hair with blue scrub hats, even our faces with masks. Offering no self-expression, we all look identical to the point we do not even recognize each other in public. Furthermore, we seldom get recognition because our encounters are asleep."

Many people feel the same way, that their job isn't the place where their creativity flourishes but is pushed aside. Angela brings her creativity out in every other way outside of work. She plants a garden and tries out new recipes, such as making homemade vinegar, yogurt, and beer. She reads about inventions in medicine. The more she wanders about things in her daily life the more she reads about it, which leads her to know a lot more about the world around her.

She even breeds goat families, using their milk to make milk and cheese. She read about similar ventures then created her own business selling her goat milk soap. "Creating these self-reliance skills gives me confidence and courage. I observe the nature around me then I want to hike the whole woods. I build swings and small houses out in my woods. I see a bobcat hit on my country road and in admiring its beauty, I read and learn how to taxidermy so I can keep it beautiful forever." The list goes on, learning Taekwondo, shooting targets, competing and volunteer teaching at biathlons against Special Forces soldiers twice her size and half her age.

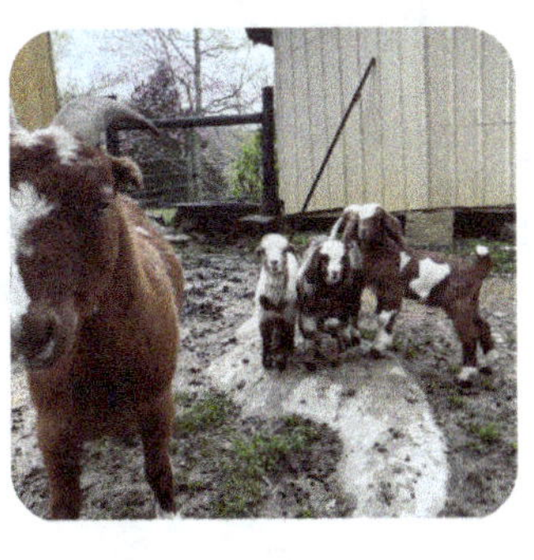

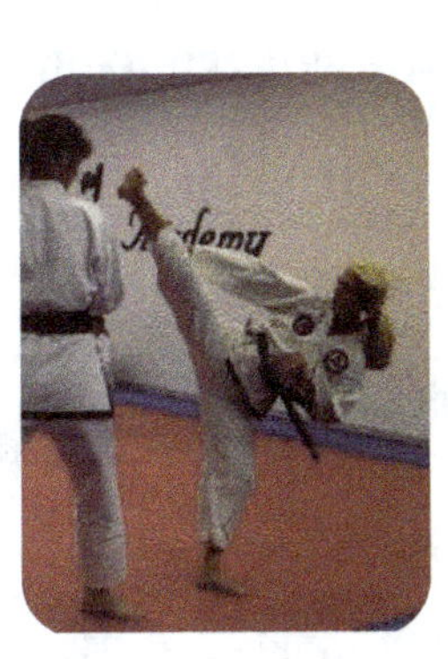

"I LOVE THE CHALLENGE, THE FEELING OF ACCOMPLISHMENT, AND CONVERSING WITH ALL TYPES OF DIFFERENT PEOPLE WITH DIFFERENT EXPERIENCES. I LEARN FROM THIS. MY BRAIN GROWS EVERY TIME I LEARN."

"It is proven that more calories are burned by reading and thinking than monotonous activity such as watching videos, scrolling posts, and gaming. Dopamine is in your brain as you expand your perception, making you happier. My heart grows from the people I encounter and volunteering opportunities."

A lot of this creativity and hardworking spirit Angela possesses comes from watching her parents as a kid. She saw friends around her dealing with hard things with the use of drugs, alcohol and bullying. The strength in saying no to such an easy relief of the pain and struggles of growing up was thinking to herself "I would not hurt my parents by taking that easy road."

"OUR PARENTS STARTED WITH NOTHING, WORKED HARD FOR EVERYTHING, HELD THEIR VALUES THE HIGHEST OF ANYTHING DESPITE LIFE CHALLENGES, AND HELD THE SURPASSING GOAL OF THEIR THREE GIRLS' HAPPINESS."

And instead of turning to other vices, Angela turned to creativity to deal with her stress. That creativity stemmed from watching her mother make her Halloween costumes as a kid and her father fixing cars, houses, or his daughter's jewelry with simple objects lying around the house. "He could make anything work again by being creative. Struggles and the lack of money and resources probably helped develop our creativity as well. Creativity equals thinking, problem-solving, and innovation for a community."

When initiating creativity now as an adult, Angela starts by viewing things as a challenge for her to overcome. She always has more confidence in doing something once she starts and feels good about the work she has done. When she is stuck on doing something, it is usually because of lack of sleep, eating unhealthily, not exercising, stressing about something, or letting someone bother her. These are things that lead everyone to procrastination. Angela knows how to pick herself up and get back on track. If she gets stuck, she tells herself to go to bed, to revisit the topic tomorrow when she has a clearer mind and is better rested.

"I do think creativity is in all of us. You just have to keep an open mind to finding it. Also, you cannot be scared to venture out on a limb and be different from everyone. Creativity is a unique expression of oneself. It is scary to put yourself out there for everyone to see who you truly are and be susceptible to judgment and reticule. Plus, there is the risk of project failure and let-down, which happens. I get extremely nervous about starting a project. Often it is difficult to take that first step."

From her reading, Angela has discovered that most medical discoveries have been born because of creativity to overcome obstacles. And in her job, creativity is seen in many ways, but her favorite is the way creativity is shown to overcome obstacles in order to obtain the comfort of children with disabilities. It is up to nurses to calm down young, scared kids. One way being, giving them a stuffed bear dressed in a surgical gown, hat, and shoes and putting a cast on it, similar to the ones kids receive in the hospital.

"IT'S A LITTLE RAY OF SUNSHINE IN THEIR STORM."

Angela, herself, wishes she had learned confidence earlier. "I feel that is my struggle in life. I have learned you have to believe in yourself, invest in yourself, and constantly grow aspects of yourself to empower against the human's ever-growing presence of self-abuse, evil and idleness."

As for social media, there are several aspects that scare her. "It scares me imagining growing up with childhood challenges and social media access. As the brain is not fully developed until age 25, vigilant supervision is required for adolescent social media use time and quality." As a nurse who witnesses the outcome of social media in many different ways, we can trust her opinion.

Even in knowing all this, Angela herself gets pulled into social media as well. She watches TikToks, feeling as most people feel on social media, the feelings of depression watching people who are so beautiful, young, happy, rich, and popular.

"IT IS DIFFICULT EVEN FOR A CONFIDENT ADULT WITH SELF-CONTROL TO REMEMBER THAT THEY ARE FILTERED AND UNREALISTIC."

But she also sees the extremely positive sides of social media. For exmaple, creating a Nurse Educator group on Facebook for educational videos or readings, a place to communicate, congratulating, inviting, and encouraging fellow nurses. Pinterest inspires her to try new recipes and make new crafts. She does think it is important for everyone to have limits on social media in order to keep a productive, happy, and healthy life.

"I feel the opportunity for calm boredom can offer great self-reflection and an objective view of your life and goals. If you overfill your head with useless monotonous activity, you distract yourself from reality and never take time to form a holistic objective view on your life and its purpose. Time will pass quickly without your paralleling growth and when you do finally have the time and boredom to reflect, you then have regrets

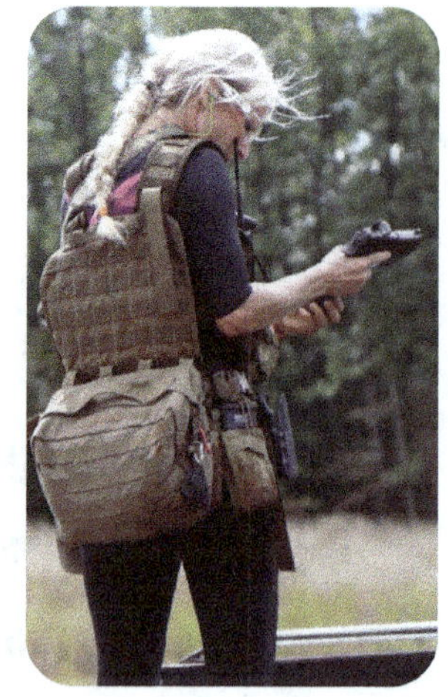

and lack self-pride from life accomplishments and growth from productive struggle. The human brain is also very adaptable. This is healthy in pinches for survival but also results in quick addictions to harmful things at times. Humans have an inherent need to belong to the group which increases the ease of addiction to social media."

"Look for something to do." -Michael B.

Michael is retired so now his main focus is enjoying life and taking care of his family. He now has time to really explore those talents, hobbies, and interests. And when I asked him what he does when he is bored he replied very simply, "Look for something to do."

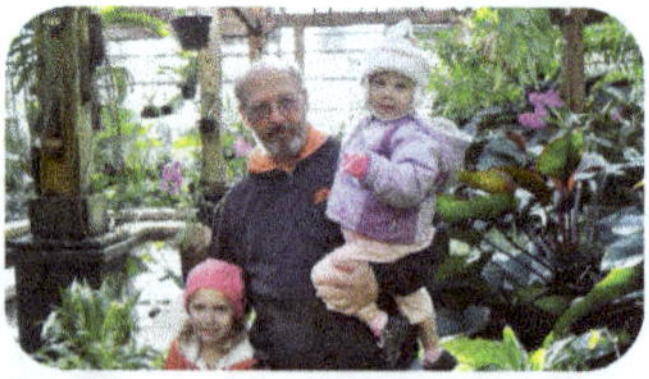

This is a very honest answer. Although a lot of people settle down when they retire, Michael has done nothing like that. Not only does he now have more time for his family, but also his friends and to do things he loves, like cross stitching, painting, or golfing.

So when I asked him if he thinks boredom can be a good thing he said, "Yes - I believe your mind and body needs some time to focus on what you have done and explore what you might do in the future. Without some occasional times with nothing to do, you would not have the time to work out problems, plan ahead, and think of new possibilities."

When it comes to painting, Michael says he spends a lot of time finding a good subject to paint. He wants to find something that people will enjoy looking at, something that he can do justice interpreting and make it the best it can be. A lot of his paintings include people he loves or pictures he takes of the world around him.

"THE CREATIVITY COMES FROM WITHIN YOU – ONLY YOU CAN FIND THE PATH THAT PULLS IT OUT. OPEN MINDS REALLY HELP THAT PROCESS."

He says that whenever you are going about any new project, it is important to know and understand the tools to do it. In doing this, you can make the project the best it can be and be proud of what you accomplish. A break from what you are working on is good, healthy even. Taking a step back can help you reevaluate and refresh which can make your final project look more polished.

Because Michael spends so much time with this creativity in his mind, social media plays an extremely small role in his everyday life. And that is how he likes it. In his eyes, social media robs your individuality and reality. This can be true. If you spend too much time looking at other people's lives, you start to envy them and even take steps to make your life more like theirs. While that can sometimes be good, it can also make you lose yourself or make you feel like who you are isn't good enough.

"I'D RATHER SEE AND ENJOY THE WORLD THROUGH MY UNFILTERED EYES."

"Our minds are truly wonderful creations that allow us to be creative in so many ways. Holding your head up and looking at this wonderful world, both the good and the bad, allows you to develop and frame your creativity with what you actually see, as opposed to what others want you to see on a screen."

"Outside my comfort zone"

-Natalie C.

Natalie is a 10th grade student. Because she is in the midst of her high school years, social media is constantly around her throughout her day. She sees the ups and the downs just like each high schooler.

Natalie told me how social media can lead the people around her into self-esteem issues. Though she has never been bullied on it, she says that if she were she would delete that app and take a step back from social media. One of Natalie's favorite things is to spend time with her family

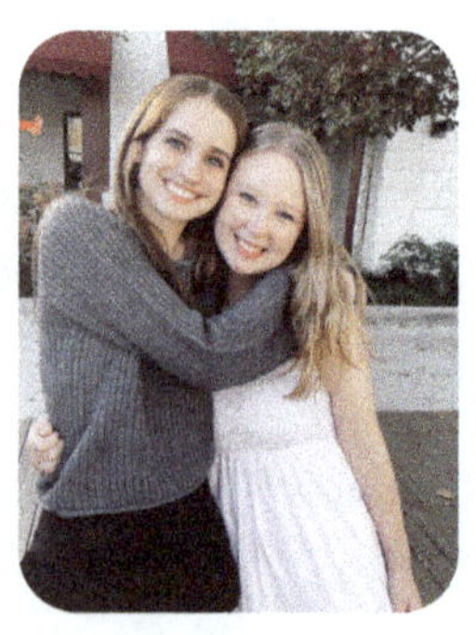

and friends so if anything on social media ever got her down, she has a good support system behind her.

Like many people her age, Natalie thinks social media is great. She told me that it is one of the main inspirations for the clothes or goods that she buys.

"I AM VERY INCLINED TO PURCHASE SOMETHING THAT IS TRENDING OR IF I SAW IT ON A POPULAR POST."

And many people do the exact same thing. Social media influencers create merch and have so many brand deals because of people like Natalie. A lot more people do this than you would think. Many people love to do it because it is like watching a commercial on your favorite app with some of your favorite influencers.

Speaking of this, Natalie loves to look around the world and see creativity around her. Things like murals, buildings, sculptures, digital art, and dance make her appreciate the world around her and the people that surround her creating these pieces of art.

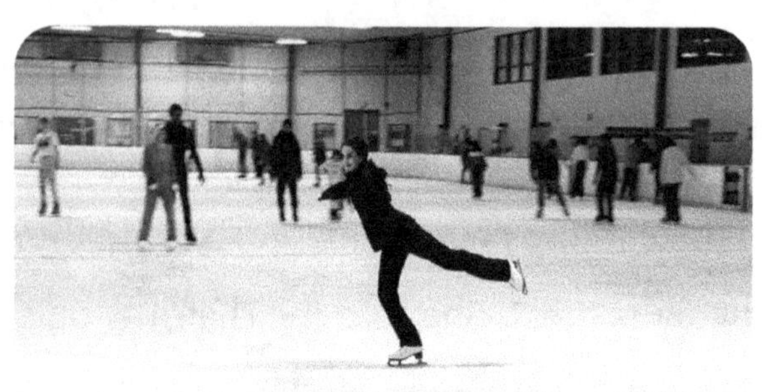

"I AM MOST PROUD OF DOING ANYTHING THAT'S OUTSIDE MY COMFORT ZONE. FOR EXAMPLE, PARTICIPATING IN A FIGURE SKATING COMPETITION WAS A CHALLENGE FOR ME, BUT IT WAS WORTH THE REWARD AND FEELING AFTERWARDS."

This is a commonly shared feeling. It is scary to break out of that comfort zone, but when you do, it feels so good, and you will want to do it more often.

Natalie says she does wish she didn't procrastinate as much as she does, "I plan to get better at that by doing my work or whatever I need to do as soon as possible, or doing it before I can go on my phone."

She starts these projects by looking up some inspiration whether that is ideas or pictures that will help her begin that process. Once she decides to start, she picks the easiest thing to get her started and then works her way up to the harder tasks till the project is finished.

"When boredom strikes"
-Kaitlin M.

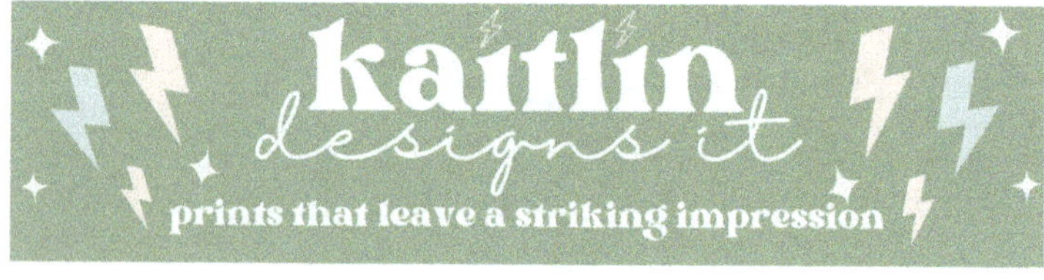

Kaitlyn M. grew up never being into anything too creative. She liked art and crafts and even took an art class in high school but never took it seriously until her final year of college when she discovered her secret talent and love for graphic design. Once she discovered her hidden talent, she turned that into getting a job focused on social media management, creating social media posts through Powerpoint or PicMonkey.

"WHAT SURPRISED ME WAS HOW MUCH I ENJOYED IT, ALBEIT MY PENCHANT FOR PERFECTIONISM SOMETIMES EXTENDED MY CREATIVE PROCESS."

After that first job, her passion grew. Creating birthday invitations through Canva or projects for family and friends became how she expressed this until making the bold leap into Etsy. Her shop had a slow start, but later that year she had 1,000 sales and 45K views on her shops, which would grow through the years following. She researches her target audience to be sure she is getting the right things out to the people on her shop.

"UNDERSTANDING MY TARGET AUDIENCE, TRENDS, AND COMPETITORS HELPS ME BRAINSTORM IDEAS THAT WILL STAND OUT."

Her job in every way is extremely creative. But when she gets bored, she uses that time to brainstorm new Etsy shop ideas or refresh the old ones. "Speaking from firsthand experience, I firmly believe that a little boredom can spark some of the most creative ideas. In fact, the origin of my Etsy shop can be traced back to a rainy Saturday, when a lack of plans led me to kick off on a creative journey!"

She recognizes that a lot of the designs she thinks are a waste of time, turn into one of her best-sellers. When those times come when she can't get motivated to work on a design, she takes a step back and works on something else. During that time she often comes up with improvements to the design whether a color scheme, word phrase, or song. Normal things inspire her work to become extraordinary, giving them a special taste or normality while at the same time make it pop. Kaitlin believes there is no limit to creativity and everyone has different tastes.

"IF YOU LIKE IT, THEN MAKE IT. IF YOU DON'T LIKE WHAT YOU MAKE, KEEP GOING UNTIL YOU DO. I GENUINELY BELIEVE CREATIVITY KNOWS NO BOUNDS."

Kaitlin learned through this entire process that finding the right balance between perfecting every detail and meeting deadlines is essential. "It is better to submit good work on time than to chase perfection and miss your due date."

As far as social media goes, Kaitlin knows what a big effect it has had on her job and her life as she knows it, calling it a "powerful tool."

"A COMPANY'S ENTIRE IMAGE CAN THRIVE OR DIVE BASED ON ITS DIGITAL FOOTPRINT..."

Her trick is to leave her phone in a different room when doing something else, so she can fully focus on her loved ones or other projects. Any form of business online is a good and healthy way to use social media to Kaitlin. Setting clear intentions and boundaries helps to keep time on social media down even if it is for business.

"FOR EXAMPLE, SOMETIMES I WILL OPEN FACEBOOK FOR THE SOLE PURPOSE OF CHECKING OUR BUSINESS ACCOUNT MESSAGES AND POST ENGAGEMENTS. AFTER THAT, I CLOSE OUT THE APP."

She also notes that a lot of her family lives away from her and social media is a great way to connect with them. She says she handles it by assigning herself one thing on social media and getting off once she completes it. But to Kaitlin, knowing if you are spending too much time on social media is really up to you.

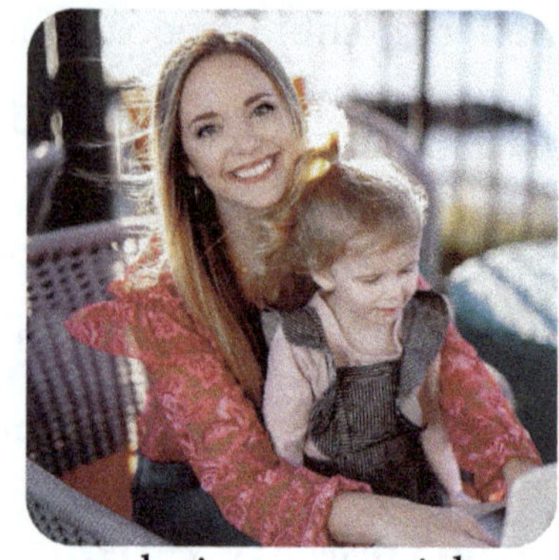

Kaitlin shared that to get where she is today she learned, researched and adapted to eventually discover the ever-changing formula to be successful. Creativity is different to each person with no limit. If you fail, don't be afraid to keep going.

"Always something that needs to be done"

-Daren T.

Daren is a retired veteran with a lot of life experience and a lot that has to be done. With life-long financial planning, he planned it well enough that right now, he doesn't really have to work.

"This is mostly made possible from the fact for the first 20 years of my adult life I almost never wasted money on a vacation. I borrowed money for my first car when I was 18. After a year of making payments and realizing just how much money I was wasting, I sold the car for what I owed on it. That was the last time I owed money on anything but land. I bought a car for $75 that I drove for four years. For the last 30 years, I have paid cash for and most of my vehicles made money when I was done fixing them up and using them for years. I am one car payment away from requiring a job. "

He worked really hard for years and that hard work paid off. He worked for the Kentucky Transportation Cabinet for 20 years and that job brought along many opportunities to be creative that most people wouldn't think of.

"I have had to get fully loaded salt trucks out of the ditch and sometimes flopped over on their side. These same trucks would generally have bent frames and other damage that we repaired creatively using high lifts and road graders to bend metal back into shape. Numerous times I have had to get equipment out of the roadway with each time being

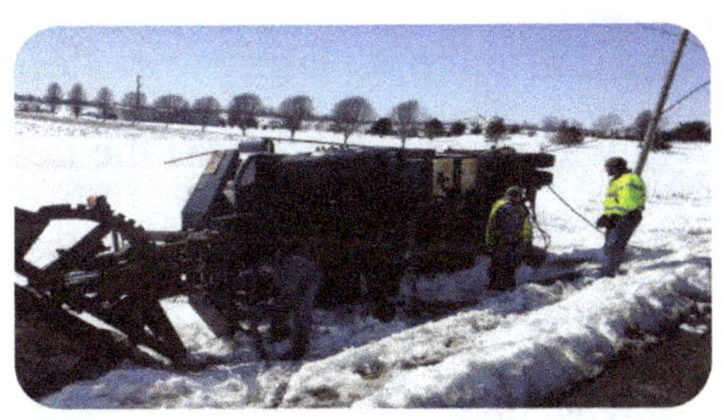

generally completely unique and requiring creative out of the box thinking. Generally, this was a team effort."

Even with no job at the moment, Daren is rarely bored. He and his wife live on 50 acres and there is always something that needs to be done.

"I THINK LONG TERM BOREDOM IS A NEGATIVE THING. IT SHOWS A LACK OF TRYING. SHORT TERM BOREDOM? WELL, THAT IS JUST WHAT HAPPENS WHEN YOU GET CAUGHT UP A BIT AND ARE WAITING FOR THINGS TO BE DELIVERED."

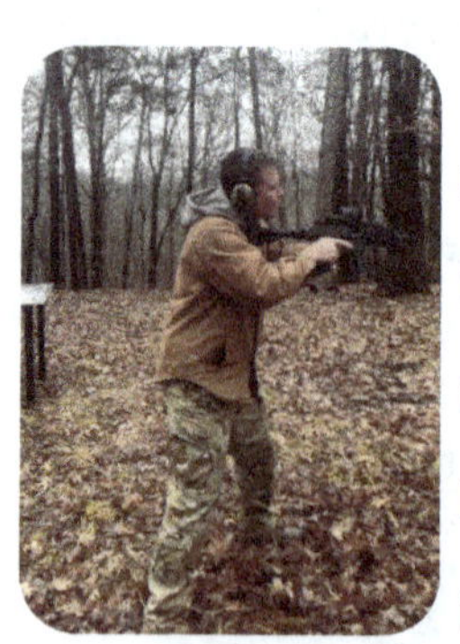

Daren grew up working for a rancher in Montana. He worked for a man, at just the age of 12 that was a Vietnam Navy veteran. Doing this taught him the importance of getting work done quickly and efficiently. He worked there for the next 4 years until the man moved and Daren started a job at a grocery store which, compared to what he was doing before, was extremely easy.

These lessons he learned in his first job stuck with him. He finds it easier to just start projects right off the bat. He says that when you just start, everything will come to you eventually. Daren says that if you never get started, you will never get done.

"PLENTY OF TIMES YOU MAY EVEN WIPE OUT EVERYTHING YOU STARTED AND DO IT OVER A DIFFERENT WAY. IT'S JUST PART OF THE PROCESS, AT LEAST FOR ME."

And when it comes to social media, Daren agrees that there is a plus and a minus to social media just like everything else in the world. It is a great place to sell things that sometimes people wouldn't even think to buy. But it brings a lot of danger as well involving the government into people's personal lives sometimes.

Daren does not have any social media accounts and if he ever goes on it, it is on his wife's accounts to either read about history on Facebook or look at the Marketplace.

Conclusion

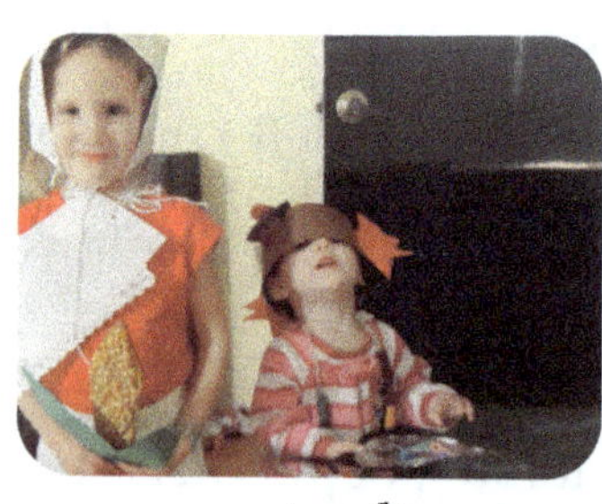

When I was little, my sister, my cousins, and I would make up plays. Whether it was acting out Taylor Swift songs, pretending we were characters in Disney movies, or using something we saw from our day and expanding on what we thought was going on. As little kids do, we would spend all day perfecting these little skits, then show them to our families, extremely proud of ourselves for what we created.

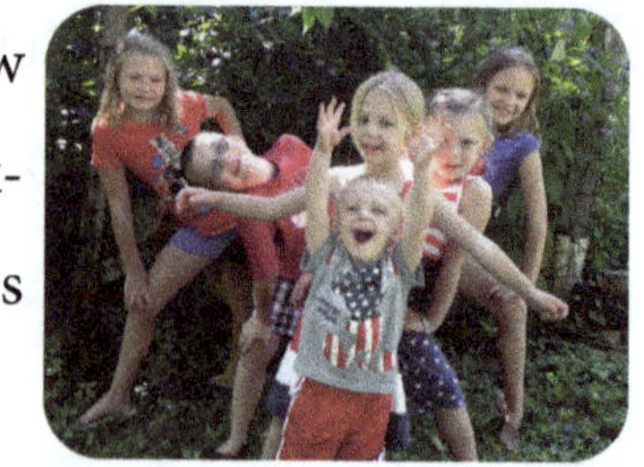

What we didn't know was that those moments were so crucial for our growing up. Even my tiny role as the wind while my sister got to be Olaf, taught us the importance of creativity. Traits like this could lead any of us to becoming actors, dancers, screenwriters or authors. My sister sitting me down, forcing me to be the student while she played teacher for hours eventually led her into going to college as an elementary education major. My four-year-old cousin making us play the customer at Chick-fil-A while she takes our order, makes the food, and has me pay her in the form of leaves, could possibly mean she will work at or own a Chick-fil-A in her future.

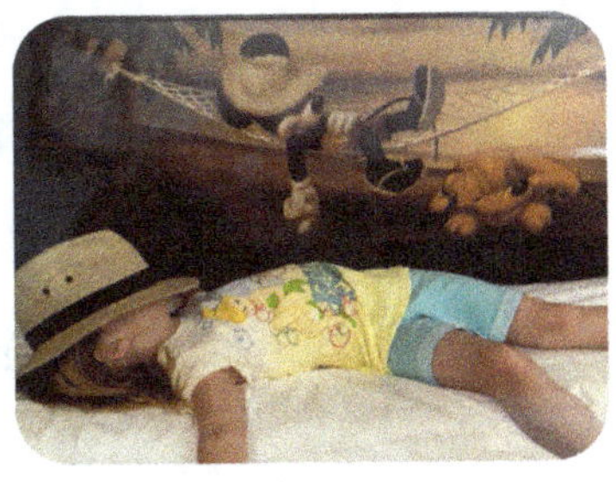

While we don't see that at her age, it is so clear to me now what it all means. We are born with a set of passions and interests we express starting before we can even comprehend what we are doing. I have always loved music. My grandma used to take thousands of videos of me just singing every word of every song that came on. I took that passion and learned guitar and now I know how to play those songs myself. You can do so much with these passions you were gifted with, but it is hard to discover exactly what those passions are.

I didn't know I would like playing guitar so much until I saw other people doing it and I realized that would be a really cool thing to do with some of my spare time. A lot of the people in this book will go off and find something new that they will end up loving and spend a lot of time doing later. For right now, this is what they are doing.

I hope that you will learn something through this book, as I learned so much while interviewing and writing it. Looking through all of these people's stories has given me a lot of time to reflect about how I ultimately spend my time. I really enjoyed writing this book, deciding exactly how I wanted the cover, the fonts and creating the perfect title. Creativity isn't really so hard to find. I am so grateful for

each person that gave up their time and gave us a glimpse of their life. And as one of my favorite books perfectly sums this all up, "Find what you love and let it kill you."
- *Verity*, Colleen Hoover

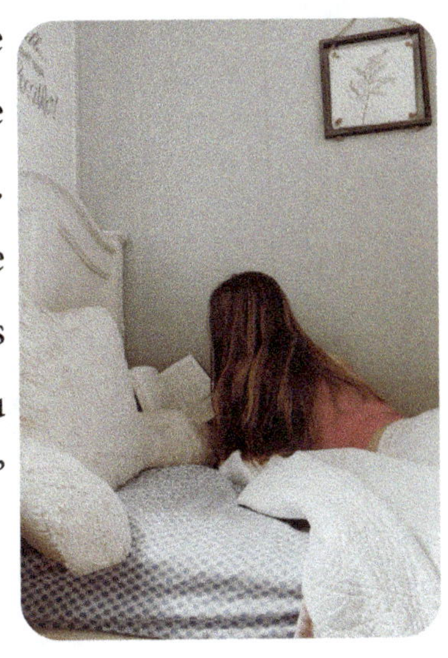

Final Thoughts

I do need to take a minute to address another reason I wrote this book. Social media addiction is a dangerously serious problem that, unfortunately, many teenagers get pulled into. This has expanded to become a global problem that does not have a current reachable cure due to its uniquely situational nature as each person has a personalized point of view and experience. While it may seem unclear to you, anyone around you could be struggling. I wrote this book in the method of voicing different individual's perspectives, through hearing their stories and thoughts, to demonstrate the effect it can have finding someone to resonate with your feelings and resulting in averting that feeling of loneliness. Though I did my best to highlight the good and bring out the fun in everyone's stories, it is good to fully understand the risks of what can happen without finding and utilizing this creativity and dare to have willingness to put yourself out there.

So much good can happen from social media but it is necessary to limit yourself so that goodness remains. Everyone has different coping mechanisms to what is going on in their lives and it is difficult to find someone who understands you in that way. Below is a QR code that will lead you to a form where you can tell me a bit about what you gained from my book. I wrote this book for my Girl Scout Gold Award project and it is important to me that people understood the goal I entended to accomplish.

In 7th grade, I completed my Girl Scout Silver Award. I wrote and illustrated a children's book about my dog, Spot, and her journey to my family. It highlights the importance of animal adoption and rescuing through the Humane Society. After I partnered with The Atlanta Humane Society and Purina to make an article and video in *The Washington Post* to share my story and promote animal adoption. The book is on Amazon called *A Spot To Call Home* and truly made me realize how important creativty is needed. If you would like to check it out here are the links to the Amazon page for *A Spot to Call Home* and *The Washington Post* article and video.

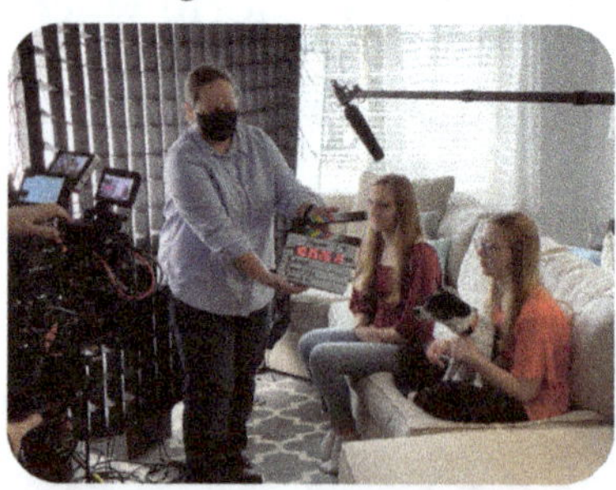

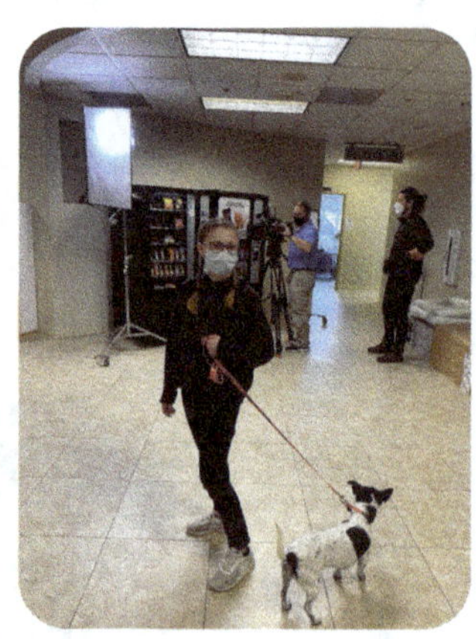

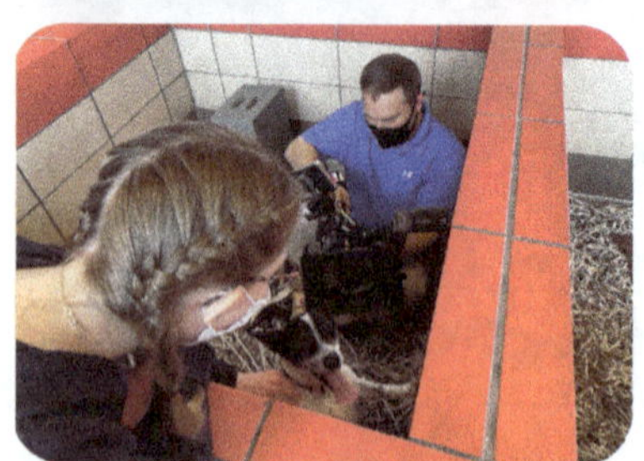

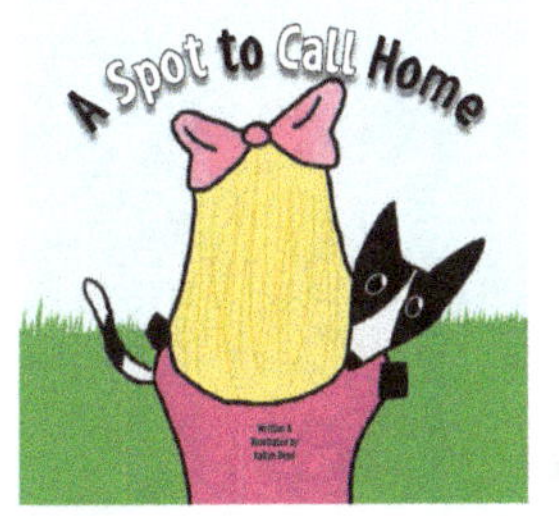

A Spot To Call Home
Amazon.com Link

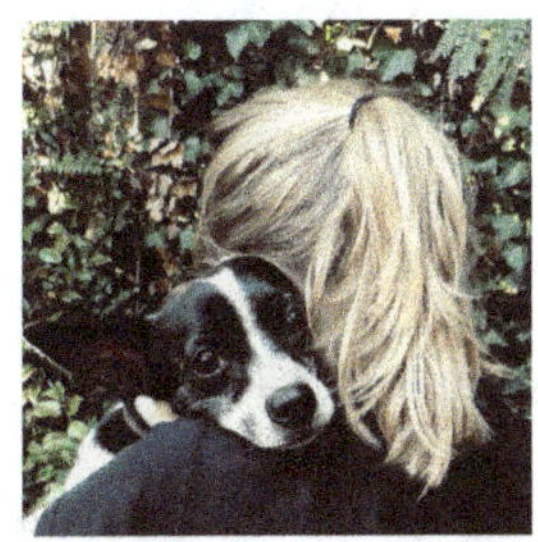

***Washington Post* / Purina**
Story on Kailyn & Spot

Acknowledgments

I would like to thank all of the people who took the time to be a part of this book, it means the world to me and to everyone who needed these stories. A huge thank you to my biggest supporters: my family. My parents, I owe everything to, especially this book. For my big sister for always being there and encouraging me to do things I am scared to do. My grandparents who support me throughout everything. My aunts, uncles, cousins, you have raised me and taught me fun. Thank you so much to my friends, whether I have known you my whole life or a second, each one of you are crucial to my life as I now know it.

To all the people in Girl Scouts who believed in me. To my aunt, Angela, who has inspired me my whole life and has completely made this book possible. Each person I love inspires me in different ways every day and I am so beyond happy that you have the opportunity to be inspired by them as well. Thank you to every author who wrote a book I fell into. And to my dog, Spot, who is always by my side on a boring day.

www.ingramcontent.com/pod-product-compliance
Lightning Source LLC
LaVergne TN
LVHW020510100826
845148LV00003B/751
9798218361921